A Psalm For Every Sigh

Finding Your Song
In God's Word

Stephen M. Crotts

CSS Publishing Company, Inc., Lima, Ohio

A PSALM FOR EVERY SIGH

Copyright © 2008 by
CSS Publishing Company, Inc.
Lima, Ohio

All rights reserved. No part of this publication may be reproduced in any manner whatsoever without the prior permission of the publisher, except in the case of brief quotations embodied in critical articles and reviews. Inquiries should be addressed to: Permissions, CSS Publishing Company, Inc., 517 South Main Street, Lima, Ohio 45804.

Scripture quotations are from the Revised Standard Version of the Bible, copyrighted 1946, 1952 ©, 1971, 1973, by the Division of Christian Education of the National Council of the Churches of Christ in the USA. Used by permission.

Scripture marked (KJV) are from the King James Version of the Bible, in the public domain.

Library of Congress Cataloging-in-Publication Data

Crotts, Stephen M.
   A psalm for every sigh : finding your song in God's word / Stephen M. Crotts.
   p. cm.
   ISBN 0-7880-2548-1 (perfect bound : alk. paper)
   1. Bible. O.T. Psalms—Meditations. I. Title.

BS1430.54.C75 2008
223'.206—dc22

2008018918

For more information about CSS Publishing Company resources, visit our website at www.csspub.com or email us at csr@csspub.com or call (800) 241-4056.

Cover design by Barbara Spencer
ISBN-13: 978-0-7880-2548-8
ISBN-10: 0-7880-2548-1

PRINTED IN USA

To Rhett Leonard,
Friend

There is something about the outside of a horse that is good for the inside of a man!
— Attributed to Ronald Reagan

Table Of Contents

Introduction	7
Psalm 1 **Nowhere Man?**	9
Psalm 2 **What Sort Of World Is This?**	19
Psalm 8 **How To Be Happy In An Unhappy World**	23
Psalm 19 **Directions Included**	31
Psalm 23:1-3 **Intensive Care — Part One**	37
Psalm 23:4-6 **Intensive Care — Part Two**	45
Psalm 27 **At Peace In A Fearful World**	53
Psalm 32 **Am I *That* Forgiven?**	59
Psalm 42 **Blowing Away The Clouds Of Depression**	65
Psalm 46; Matthew 28:16-20 **The Good Now Days!**	73
Psalm 107 **No More Stingy Hosannas**	81

Psalm 120   89
    Forward, Retreat!

Psalm 126   97
    How To Heal With Humor

Psalm 127   107
    The Mattress Gospel

Psalms 120-134   117
    Getting Away From It All To Get Back To It All

Afterword   125

Introduction

The psalms make up the heart of the Bible. In the Hebrew language, a psalm is a poem set to music. It is to touch the strings, twanging and musing upon the harp — the most complete utterance. The book of Psalms is the most quoted book in the New Testament. It is the book Jesus Christ drew from most in his teaching.

In the last 500 years, the psalms have been the best source of inspiration for classical and contemporary music, from Bach's "Sheep May Safely Graze" to the praise chorus "As The Deer Pants For The Water."

The collection of psalms begins with Psalm 1 and introduces us to two sorts of people: the godly and the godless. The one lives life in reference to God. The other lives life on his own terms. The next 148 psalms show us these two sorts of people living their lives through all manners of situations.

Psalm 150, the final psalm, tells one how to use the book. It basically answers who, where, how, and what.

- What? "Praise the Lord."
- Where? In and out of the temple.
- How? With music, dance, loudly, and quietly. And it mentions eight different musical instruments!
- Who? "All with breath" should praise the Lord.

The book of Psalms was meant to be sung to the accompaniment of instruments. However, the music has long since been lost, for sheet music has only been around 500 years, and these psalms are over 2,500 years old. The Geneva Psalter set each psalm to music 500 years ago. Many contemporary choruses render some of the psalms beautifully.

When I was a youth, I read the psalms and thought, "What is this person groaning about so much?" Now that I am old, I read them and say, "How sublime are his yearnings!"

It has been said, "There is a psalm for every sigh." Yes, there is a psalm for praise — Psalm 34:1-5, a psalm for nature — Psalm

19:1-2, a psalm of confession — Psalm 32, a psalm of gratitude — Psalm 100, a psalm of depression — Psalm 42, and a psalm of old age — Psalm 71:17-18. There are psalms for vacationers — the psalms of sweet ascent — Psalms 120 through 134. Even some psalms rail against one's enemies — Psalm 3.

The point is that worship is not stuck in one gear. Just as celebration is a legitimate part of our worship experience, so is lament, confession, quietness, and reflection.

John Wesley said it well in observing certain Christians of his day. "Strange that a man with a harp of 10,000 strings should pluck on so few strings." Certain Christians of our own day likewise do not give the harp its full voice. They are seemingly stuck in celebration mode or the judgment mode. Authentic Christian worship, however, is musical, even poetic, and its moods are myriad.

A few years ago, with a group of theology students, I visited Buchenwald, a Nazi concentration camp near Weimar, Germany. Oh, the human depravity, man's inhumanity to man! I put my hand on the oven door handle where corpses were incinerated. We left to drive to Leipzig. It was a somber drive, each of us lost in thought over the human predicament.

In Leipzig, we went to St. Thomas Church, where J. S. Bach is buried. As providence would have it, a Bach concert of psalms with trumpet and organ was just starting. For an hour, the music of Christ's praise filled the nave. Our spirits were lifted. The psalms have been ministering like that to people for centuries.

Bach wrote, "All music should have no other end and aim than the glory of God and the soul's refreshment. When this is not remembered, there is no real music, but only a devilish hubbub."

Do you realize that the Judeo-Christian faith is the only religion with a hymn book? We have something — *someone* — to sing about!

The following are expositions of some of the psalms. They've touched my life and enriched my worship. My prayer is that they will do the same for you.

— Stephen M. Crotts
Chapel Hill, North Carolina
Spring 2008

Psalm 1

Nowhere Man?

Blessed is the man who walks not in the counsel of the wicked, nor stands in the way of sinners, nor sits in the seat of scoffers; but his delight is in the law of the Lord, and on his law he meditates day and night. He is like a tree planted by streams of water, that yields its fruit in its season, and its leaf does not wither. in all that he does, he prospers.

The wicked are not so, but are like chaff which the wind drives away. Therefore the wicked will not stand in the judgment, nor sinners in the congregation of the righteous; for the Lord knows the way of the righteous, but the way of the wicked will perish. — Psalm 1

In Greek, *psalm* means "twanging upon the strings." In Hebrew, it means "a poem set to notes" or "to strike the strings." Sometimes the psalms are called "the Book of Shining Forth."

Actually, the psalms are the hymn and prayer book of Israel. Jesus was familiar with the book, quoting from it with frequency, and at least once, after the Last Supper, he sang from it with his disciples (Matthew 26:30).

In the Bible, almighty God is saying, "Here I am! Look at me! This is what I'm like, how I think, what I do. Turn to me and live abundantly forever!" The psalms are man's response to such a God.

When I was younger and read the psalms, I thought to myself, "What's this fellow groaning about so much?" Now that I am older, however, I read the psalms and marvel at how articulately he expresses my own feelings to God.

It's been said, "There is a psalm for every sigh," and indeed there are. Some psalms share feelings of failure, depression, fear of enemies, and doubt. Others are about victory, joy, gratitude, worship, and war.

Today we hear the Top 40 "Hit Parade" on the radio. The psalms are 150 of Israel's best worship songs over the centuries and Psalm 1 is number one on their hit parade. Being the introductory song, Psalm 1 is the key to understanding the entire book. Basically, it describes two different types of people — horizontal people and vertical people.

Horizontal People

Let's look at the horizontal man first. You may recall a popular Beatles song from the 1970s titled, "Nowhere Man." The words may be found online. It speaks of a person without plans and without a point of reference for his life. He is lost. This represents many in today's world.

The horizontal man is such a nowhere man. The psalm describes him as a slave to peer pressure who does little more than follow the crowd and hang around with sinners.

First off, Psalm 1 says this sort of man never asks God anything. He, instead, "Walks in the counsel of the ungodly." The Hebrew word for "ungodly" actually means "loud" or "noisy." This man simply follows the clamor of society. The voice that shouts the loudest to him is the truest. For many of these people today, that is the voice of television, radio, fads, magazines, and "with it" advice columnists.

Some newspapers today carry a column called "Straight Up" by Stephen the Bartender. In it, the columnist responds to questions of sex, finances, employment, marriage, or whatever. I know a preacher who, counseling with a middle-aged housewife, was told, "*Desperate Housewives* is my favorite soap opera. I watch it every day because the leading lady's problem is the same as mine. I keep thinking that she'll show me some solutions."

The horizontal person, according to the text, also "stands in the way of sinners." He not only listens to their counsel and walks in it; he stands for what they do, votes with them, and encourages others to do so as well. Last year, I went to visit a young student who had been living with a group of peers. A near-fatal drug overdose landed him in the hospital. We talked long and freely about purpose in life, drugs, and God. I asked him if he needed anything. "No," he assured me, he'd be just fine. But as I turned to go, he said, "Stephen, there is one thing I need. When I get out of here I'm going to need a whole new set of friends."

The psalm goes on to say that this horizontal person not only walks in ungodly counsel and stands with them; he also "sits in the seat of scoffers." In other words, he makes light of values, tradition, morals, scripture, godly leadership, and the like!

At a university, an unusual experiment was conducted recently. Ten people were asked to wear a pair of reverse-lens glasses for two weeks. When put on, the spectacles turned the world upside down. The floor was the ceiling and vice versa. For fourteen days, the participants tried to function in a topsy-turvy world. Afterward they sat down to evaluate, and on one point they all agreed. How quickly they adjusted!

"Scoffers," the horizontal people the psalm describes, see the world through a kind of reverse-lens morality. To them a policeman is a "pig," a "pimp" and "pusher" are friends, the bartender is their priest, the preacher is a bore, and Mom and Dad are enemies.

Be careful to notice in the text how the nowhere man gets progressively comfortable with sin. He begins by *walking* in the counsel of the ungodly. Soon he is *standing* in the way of sinners. Finally he is *sitting* with scoffers. Do you see the gradualism there? Little by little, his life loses momentum until he is one of the noisy crowd.

I like the story of a man who was going bald. It seemed that everybody around him knew it but him. Every morning he'd wake up and there on his pillow would be dozens of his hairs. But it didn't bother him. He'd go shampoo his scalp, blow his hair dry, and comb it carefully. This went on for several years. Each morning there were more hairs on his pillow and fewer hairs on his head, until he had only three hairs left. Still, the man got up, shampooed his three hairs, blew them dry, and combed them down carefully as he'd always done. Then one day it happened. He woke up and there were his last three hairs on his pillow. Nevertheless, he went into the shower, shampooed, blew his scalp dry, took his brush in hand, and stepped over to the mirror to comb his hair. A look of utter surprise crossed his face, and he exclaimed, "It can't be! I'm going bald!"

One by one we give up our values in ways that aren't very noticeable. Little by little the changes overtake us. The months turn into years and we, who once walked vertically before God, now live entirely horizontally, even sitting comfortably in the seat of scoffers — and "how quickly we adjusted."

Where does following the noise lead? Where will peer pressure and horizontal living take you? The text gives the result in verse 4. "The wicked ... are like chaff which the wind drives away."

The picture is of a farmer who has harvested his wheat. He leaves it to dry in the sunshine, then on a windy day takes his crop to the top of a hill. With a winnowing fork, he takes a shovelful of the wheat and tosses it into the air. The wind blows the lightweight husk away while the heavier and edible grain falls back to the ground. This is repeated until the husk is gone and nothing but fine grain remains. Psalm 1 is saying that this process is going on right now in this world. God is sifting or winnowing all people, separating the wheat from the chaff.

When I was younger in ministry, I used to come home perplexed with some people's foolishness. They skipped every opportunity to learn from God, chaffed under every authority, and violated themselves against every moral principle of Christ. "What happens to people like that?" I'd often ask my wife. Now that I am older I no longer ask. The suicides, prison sentences, alcoholism, cancer, and death tell the answer all too clearly. Sinners do not endure. They, like chaff, get blown away to nowhere with the winds of time.

This part of the text actually prefigures the ministry of Jesus Christ. John the Baptist said of Jesus, "His winnowing fork is in his hand, and he will clear his threshing floor and gather his wheat into the granary, but the chaff he will burn with unquenchable fire" (Matthew 3:12).

So, the wicked shall not endure. When the grain falls, the chaff gets blown away like so much rubbish to be burned. When

Christians are gathered to God, the wicked will perish. The latter portion of the psalm spells their doom:

> *The wicked are not so, but are like chaff which the wind drives away. Therefore the wicked will not stand in the judgment, nor sinners in the congregation of the righteous; for the Lord knows the way of the righteous, but the way of the wicked will perish.* — Psalm 1:4-6

The Vertical Man

That is the lifestyle and end of the horizontal man. Now there is this — the lifestyle and fate of the vertical man.

Clearly, the vertical man does not walk, stand, sit, or otherwise hang around with sinners. He doesn't care what people say so much as he cares what God says. He is anxious to absorb God's word not the world's fads.

The psalm says, "His delight is in the law of the Lord." The Hebrew word for "delight" means to crave, to seek after with pleasure. There is a picture of this in Proverbs 2:1-15. There the vertical man "cries out for insight, raises his voice for understanding, seeks it like silver, searches for it as for hidden treasure."

Notice also the psalm says this type of person also "meditates" on God's word. Here, the Hebrew for "meditate" means "to murmur, to ponder, to chew over and over again as the cow chews his cud until it is completely digested." This means we think God's thoughts after him, we narrow our way of thinking about life to God's way of thinking.

The text goes on to say that the vertical man delights and meditates on God's word both "day and night" not just on Sundays — weekdays and Saturdays, summers, too, along with holidays. For him, his religion is not just something to be put on and taken off with his Sunday coat. It is an every hour and every day consuming delight murmured in his dreams, hummed under his breath, discussed around the supper table, and shouted aloud in his business deals.

What is the result of such a vertical lifestyle? The text says, "He is like a tree." But not just any kind of tree. The psalm says he is "planted." This means he is not a wild tree, growing at random in a chance spot, uncultivated. He is planted by God in a specific spot for a purpose.

In May of 2007, I bought a red maple tree and carefully planted it where it'd get plenty of sunshine and where I could see it from my favorite chair. The Bible is saying here that God plants us where he wants us, where we can do the most good. So, take heart! The job you find yourself in, the neighborhood, the circumstances, whatever, are not accidental because you are a vertical person who delights and meditates on God's word day and night. You are like a tree God will plant where he wants.

Continue with the psalm and notice where God plants his trees. They are not in the salt flats of some barren desert, nor on some hard rock, but "planted by streams of water."

For a fascinating study of all this, take time to look up the various things the Bible says about God's streams and rivers. Psalm 46:4 says, "There is a river whose streams make glad the city of God, the holy habitation of the most high." Psalm 36:8-9 teaches that God "gives them drink from the river of thy delights. For with thee is the fountain of life." The prophet Ezekiel saw this same river, and in chapter 47 describes it as flowing out of the temple of God, getting ever deeper and deeper, and bringing life to all along its banks. In John's gospel, Jesus identifies with this river by making the Samaritan woman abandon her water pot (John 4), by making the pool of healing at Bethesda unnecessary (John 5), by walking on water (John 6), and finally in John 7:37 by proclaiming himself a river of life: "If anyone thirsts, let him come to me and drink."

When we live vertically, we watch with whom we walk, stand, and sit with. We delight in God and meditate on his words day and night. The result is to be planted where God wants us in Jesus Christ, to have our roots in an extraordinary river of life.

Now this: We bear "fruit in its season." This fruit is not only personal character as mentioned in Galatians 5:22: "love, joy, peace, patience," and the like. It is also the fruit of ministry, the fruit of good deeds, among the people who live around us. Jesus said, "Abide in me ... by this my Father is glorified, that you bear much fruit, and so prove to be my disciples" (John 15:1-9).

Over the years, I have known some people to bear fruit and then go barren. Good things fall from their lives to others for a season, and then nothing. It's as if they are all bloomed out. But the text says this doesn't happen to the believer who has his roots in the river. He "yields his fruit in its season." That means regularly, year after year, you can count on good fruit to fall from this man's life.

"And its leaf does not wither," the psalm says. So many Christians live life like a maple tree — one day they are sap-filled and green, the next colorful, and the next barren. They are up and down like a yo-yo, in and out of ministry — on-again-off-again obeyers. One never knows if they're going to be effective or depressed, available or quitters, loving or indifferent. Yet, the vertical man in Christ, whose roots are in the river, is evergreen. While everyone about him is changing, decaying, and coming to life again, he is evergreen, always steadfast and on the grow.

Finally the text says, "In all that he does he prospers." The Hebrew word for "prosper" means "to push forward, to advance." This doesn't mean you'll necessarily get a million dollars, drive a Cadillac, and live in a palace. It means that in all you do you'll advance in God. I don't have a Swiss bank account, a yacht, or fifty servants, but God is pushing me forward into his wisdom. He's given me a house with love in it, plenty to eat, quality friends in fellowship, and meaningful work to perform. In every sense I am rich. I prosper in that my life is balanced with every good thing and I am closer to heaven than I have ever been before! All this God has done for me!

Conclusion

The horizontal man starts off walking and ends up sitting. He makes no progress. His life is at a standstill. Like chaff he gets blown away with the rubbish to nowhere. He won't stand in the judgment.

The vertical man's way is known and prospered by God. He not only has enough for himself, he has plenty for others just like a fruit tree.

You can see the vertical man pictured in Revelation.

> *There he showed me the river of the water of life, bright as crystal, flowing from the throne of God and of the Lamb through the middle of the street of the city; also, on either side of the river, the tree of life with its twelve kinds of fruit yielding its fruit each month; and the leaves of the tree were for the healing of the nations.*
> — Revelation 22:1-2

See here how God says he plants us like trees along every street? We bear twelve different types of fruit, a different one each month. The leaves that fall from us are for the healing of the nations. The books we loan, advice we give, sermons we preach, letters we write, phone calls we make, and children we rear, all fall like leaves from our lives and bring healing to others.

I find it thrilling that the first word in the book of Psalms is the word "blessed." It comes from the Hebrew which means "to cause to bow down." The picture behind it is that of a camel that kneels down so it can be loaded. This is what God wants to do for us. He wills us to bow before him in worship so he can load us down with every delight and through us bless those around us. This same idea is in Psalm 68:19: "Blessed be the Lord who daily loadeth us with benefits" (KJV).

Which type of person are you? Are you a vertical person or a horizontal person? Are you a nowhere man or a somewhere man? Are you moving toward heaven with God or sitting with scoffers? Are you a prosperous evergreen with your roots in the river or a sickly sage bush with your roots in parched soil? Are your limbs laden with different kinds of fruit and healing leaves, or full of rubbish, thorns, bad counsel, and mockery?

The prophet Jeremiah sums up life going on around us and the two different types of people living it.

> *Cursed is the man who trusts in man and makes flesh his arm, whose heart turns away from the Lord. He is like a shrub in the desert, and shall not see any good*

come. He shall dwell in the parched places of the wilderness, in an uninhabited salt land.

Blessed is the man who trusts in the Lord, whose trust is in the Lord. He is like a tree planted by water, that sends out its roots by the stream, and does not fear when heat comes, for its leaves remain green and is not anxious in the year of drought, for it does not cease to bear fruit. — Jeremiah 17:5-8

Which lifestyle will you choose?

Suggested Prayer

O, Lord Jesus Christ, I choose you! I have time for you; I choose to think your thoughts, to obey you, to bear your fruit. Amen.

Psalm 2

What Sort Of World Is This?

Why do the nations conspire and the peoples plot in vain? — Psalm 2:1

The Declaration of Independence guarantees Americans "the pursuit of happiness," and we live in the cultural scramble to attain it. Is it in marriage? Singleness? How much money does it take? Will I need a new car? A better job? Children?

The psalms have much to say here. They begin with the word, "Blessed," which means "happy, the state of utmost bliss."

Psalm 1 teaches some are happy and some are not. Vertical people live life in reference to God and are blessed. Horizontal people ignore God and disintegrate in despair.

Psalm 2 explains more of the world we live in, giving three views of earth.

1. The Nations Rage
2. God In Heaven Laughs
3. God's Children Serve Him

The conclusion? Those who take refuge in him are "blessed." There's that word again — "happy."

Let's go deeper.

Two Questions

In trying to understand his world, the psalmist asks two questions. The first is, "Why do the nations rage?" Why do big groups (nations) rage? In Hebrews, "rage" is a stormy sea, restless, roaring, and crashing. Why is there so much international conflict?

He's trying to relate faith to foreign policy. How refreshing! The poet is not just concerned with his personal health or kids or finances, but with the family of man — war, injustice, genocide, or nuclear proliferation. How can one be happy in such a world?

Today, we're a little different. If we can just get the next election to go right, if North Korea will come to the bargaining table, if we can extract our troops from the Middle East, then things will be okay, I can relax and be happy.

The second question he asks is "Why do people plot in vain?" Why do so many individuals stir through life so vainly, so emptily, so confused? Indeed! Divorce, low self-esteem, depression, joblessness, and bouncing from one religion to another — we live lives like a letter addressed to nowhere.

Three Reasons

The psalmist inquires about international conflict and individual confusion. He lists the causes for such a sorry state of affairs. He cites three:

1. There is leadership in society against God. "The kings take their stand against God."
2. There is antagonism to the lordship of Christ. "Rulers take counsel against the Lord."
3. We have a fatal attraction to lawlessness. "Let us throw off their chains."

Years ago, my three preschool children disobeyed their mother. She told them, "Just wait till your father gets home." When I drove up, I found the driveway blockaded with their toys! And the Bible is saying all humanity is in rebellion against God and his rule, and his law.

In Heaven

The psalmist looks away from this turbulent world to more serene places — to God in heaven. There he recognizes the superiority of God over all kings.

- He understands God is sovereign, in control, unrivaled.
- He sees God laughing securely as sinners try to assail his reign.
- He sees God speaking clearly his truth.
- He sees God select Messiah to sit on the throne of the universe forever.

And this sweet psalmist of Israel turns to give advice in verse 10. He writes, "Now, therefore...." It is a call to you and to me to join God in his labors. How?

We do so by warning people, "Be warned, O rulers of the earth. There is a God. You are not him."

We call people to love God with their minds — "Now, therefore, O King, be wise...."

We call people to love God with their will — "Serve the Lord with fear." We call everyone to love God emotionally — "Kiss the Son."

The result is happiness. "Blessed are all those who take refuge in him." "Refuge" means a safe place or security. In this troubled world, we find in God a dependable safety.

Conclusion

The psalm calls us from viewing our world as muddy-eyed pessimists. "Woe!" "Confusion!" "War!" "All is lost!"

Likewise, we are not starry-eyed optimists. "We can do this! Just need a little more time!"

Rather, we are balanced between the two extremes — up to our armpits in people and their problems at home, in church, and internationally. But we are looking to Christ, and to his coming, for a remedy.

Allow me to close with a question. Since Jesus is the only sovereign of the universe and he will break all pretenders like an iron rod breaks a clay pot, can he leave you or me out?

Suggested Prayer
Lord, I bow! Forgive! Rule, Lord Jesus! Amen.

Psalm 8

How To Be Happy In An Unhappy World

What is man that thou art mindful of him, and the son of man that thou dost care for him? — Psalm 8:4

*Whenever Richard Cory went down town,
We people on the pavement looked at him:
He was a gentleman from sole to crown,
Clean favored, and imperially slim.*

*And he was always quietly arrayed,
And he was always human when he talked;
But still he fluttered pulses when he said,
"Good Morning," and he glittered when he walked.*

*And he was rich — yes, richer than a king —
And admirably schooled in every grace:
In fine, we thought that he was everything
To make us wish that we were in his place.*

*So on we worked and waited for the light,
And went without the meat, and cursed the bread;
And Richard Cory, one calm summer night,
Went home and put a bullet through his head.*[1]

This poem by Edwin Arlington Robinson points to a very real problem in our society — suicide. From 1980 to the present, suicide among 15- to 24-year-olds rose 254%. This year 250,000 adolescents will attempt to kill themselves. Over 6,000 will succeed. Overall, more than 30,000 Americans will take their own lives this year.

This brings us to Psalm 8 and a study of how to be happy in an unhappy world. Note the psalm begins and ends with praise: "O Lord, our Lord, how majestic is thy name in all the earth!" But what does all of this have to do with being happy? Just this: Verse 4 asks a question, "What is man?" What is it to be human? What is it to be a person, to be me?

You see, it is impossible to be happy without a positive self-image, and the fact that so many people are destroying themselves today is strong evidence that individuals are deficient in self-esteem. Suicide is the number two killer of teenagers these days. The number one killer is accidents and most of them are alcohol-related, which points to self-esteem troubles, also. We have got a big problem!

But where does one get a positive self-image? In counseling, if you ask a grown man to tell you about himself, he'll tell you about his job. A woman will tell you about her husband and children. A teenager will tell you about his or her sports. A single person will tell you about his or her lover or his or her latest project. In every case, each person is measuring his or her own self-worth by someone or something. The trouble is, we get fired from jobs, retire from accomplishments, and children grow up and move on. Then where is our self-esteem? How do you look at who you are? How do you value yourself? Is your self-image in people — things — accomplishments — beauty? The author of Psalm 8 finds his value in God.

He Looks At God

It is a paradox, but durable self-esteem does not begin with ourselves or even with what others think of us. It begins with who God is and what he thinks of us. Psalm 8:1-2 focuses on who God is. In the entire psalm, God is mentioned nineteen times while references to people occur about nine times. The focus, you see, is on deity, not self. God is the center, not me.

"O Lord, our Lord, how majestic is thy name!" It is easy to become so impressed with self that we've no time for God. But not the author of Psalm 8, he begins with worship. He ascribes worth to God.

"O Lord, our Lord, how majestic is thy name in all the earth!" "O Lord" — the word is *Yahweh* — the word that sums up all who God is, a word so holy the Jews found it all but unspeakable. "Our Lord" — the word here is *Adonai* or "Lord" meaning the master, the ruler, or the one in charge. "How majestic is thy name" — large, imposing, permanent, as unchanging as the mountains. Then there is the word "our" — God is personal, not aloof, unavailable, or indifferent.

Then, too, his name is majestic in "all the earth." God's not just famous in two states. He is known throughout the cosmos generation after generation. "Thou whose glory is chanted ..." this refers to his weightiness, his radiance. This great God can even "still the enemy and the avenger." In other words, he can control history. He has power to begin and end, to limit and permit. Christ dying on the cross is not letting things get out of hand. Why, God actually raised him from the dead. Consider the work of his hands — "the moon and the stars." I've built an arbor over my back porch. It's a joy to have friends over and sit in the vine-covered cool and show off my workmanship. But step out from under it and look toward the canopy of space. Who could do that but God?

"O *Yahweh* our *Adonai*, how majestic is thy name in all the earth!"

All of this praise pours out in just a few verses of one psalm. Yet there is so much more to his name. In fact, trying to know and understand all of God is like trying to capture the ocean in a thimble.

I don't think we esteem God highly enough. We are so consumed with our personal misery or so preoccupied with our own cleverness that we've no time for deity. But not this author of Psalm 8. First and foremost he is overwhelmingly impressed with who God is. Second, he is impressed with creation.

He Looks At Creation

In verse 3, the psalmist looks at the moon and the stars and "considers." Is it all an accident? Did no one make these things? Is it all random, a chance dance of atoms in a universe of absurdity? Or is there a genius behind it all and perhaps behind me, too? Consider:

- Evolution says you are the product of a long, naturalistic process, one of the fittest to survive the ordeal. You have worth in your ability to dominate.
- Secularism says you are important only as you accomplish. Your self-worth, then, is measured in your achievements and acclaim.
- Marxism says you have value only as you produce. "From each according to his ability, to each according to his need." You are worth what you can do.
- Materialism says you are worth what you possess. The richer you are the more value and meaning you have.
- Nihilism says you are nothing but a sick fly taking a dizzy ride on a gigantic dirt ball hurtling through space.
- German Dadaism defines you as an absurdity. You have no meaning. Life is nonsense.

In just about every case, you have no value in and of yourself! If you have meaning and worth, it is only because you produce, achieve, possess, or dominate. This is completely different from the gospel of Jesus Christ and his definition of you. The Bible says you have worth and meaning because God made you, because you are created in his image.

If you will, consider, for a moment, that bane of the household — the common fly. Have you ever seen one walk across your ceiling and wonder how he does it? Why doesn't gravity pull him down? Does he have claws? Actually, it's all done with glue. Attached to each of a fly's legs are dozens of tiny, hollow hairs with a sack of glue at each end. When a fly alights, pressure is exerted and through each hollow hair a bit of glue is secreted that gives its feet sticking power.

Just look at a fly's radar system and its maneuvering ability in flight — all that comes from a pin-head-sized brain! Why, if I could manufacture such an amazing aircraft for the Air Force I'd have a contract worth billions! Yet, a fly can reproduce itself by the millions! And what is its fuel? High-grade jet fuel? No, almost any waste will do. Such is the creation of God!

The amazing thing is that if I kill a fly, God is not in the least angry with me. He's got billions of others!

Go on! Consider "the moon and the stars." I recall a United States astronaut who landed on the moon. He said he was really beginning to feel like a big shot until he started home and saw the earth the size of a basketball floating alone in an awesome vastness. Suddenly he realized just how small he was.

Consider on! Psalm 8 mentions babies and angels, but finally one's own self. "What is man that thou art mindful of him?" As extraordinary as the housefly is, as spectacular as is outer space, the human species is more amazing still. In Psalm 139, the author describes himself as being "fearfully and wonderfully made." Centuries ago, Augustine wrote, "Men travel abroad to see mountains and cities, to marvel at great oceans, and all the while miss the marvels of themselves."

Consider yourself — you're God's creation, made in his image! Consider taste, touch, smell, and hearing. Don't forget sight. What a work is man! "O Lord, our Lord, how majestic is thy name in all the earth!"

So far, the poet has shown us that he is very impressed with who God is and what his creation is like. Now he looks at himself, and there he finds something impressive as well.

He Looks At Himself

First, perhaps, the psalmist tilts toward an inferiority complex. In verse 4 he compares himself to God and the rest of creation and moans, "What is man that thou art mindful of him?" Hear that? "I don't matter. No one cares if I live or die. I'm single, unloved. I've got the personality of a dial tone. Today the boss fired me. See there? That just goes to prove how worthless I am."

Emily Dickinson has a poem with something of this pain in it. It is titled "I'm Nobody! Who are you?" It can be found online at http://www.poets.org/viewmedia.php/prmMID/15392.

You can find some of this in the Charlie Brown comic strip, as well. Charlie is talking to his friend, Linus, about the pervasive sense of inadequacy he feels all the time. Charlie moans, "You see, Linus, it goes all the way back to the beginning. The moment I was born and set foot on the stage of life they took one look at me and said, 'Not right for the part.'"

"What is man that thou art mindful of me?" "I don't count! I'm so worthless! Just one big mistake!" And a low estimation of oneself is dangerously close to insulting God. For we are actually thinking lowly of something he made.

Note that the psalmist tilts toward the other extreme. From an inferiority complex he now leans toward a superiority complex. In verse 5 he muses, "Yet Thou hast made me little less than God, and dost crown me with glory and honor."

On television's game show, *Wheel of Fortune*, the host comes on stage to a thunderous applause. He bows and says immodestly, "I know, I feel the same way, too!" And so it is with many of us. We're impressed with ourselves to the point of conceitedness.

But the psalmist finds a balance between an inferiority complex and a superiority complex. He can say with real honesty, "What am I?" But he can say with just as genuine a passion, "Thou hast made me little less than God and put all things under my feet." He can mention God nineteen times in this single psalm, but not forget to mention himself ten or eleven times, as well. His self-esteem is simply held in this tension. So ours must be, as well.

When someone asks, "Stephen, tell me about yourself," I can answer, "I am a creation of God. He has fearfully and wonderfully made me! I am unique among the people of the world, the only one of my kind! No one else has my fingerprints! Just as the telephone company took seven digits and made a special number for each person, so God took hair, race, sex, teeth, eyes, temperaments, and talents and made me what I am right now. He knows my name. Why, the very hairs of my head are numbered."

In the New Testament book of Hebrews, chapter 2, Psalm 8 is quoted as describing Jesus Christ. This is a reminder that we have fallen so short of what we were created to be that God had to come and redeem us by dying on the cross for our sins. Look at the cross — it is not an "X" negating our self-worth, but a kind of divine plus mark affirming our value. God is saying, "I'm willing to hurt for you! I count you worthy of this!"

The good news gets better. When we respond to Christ, he tells us he wants to take us as his bride to live with him for all eternity! Until then, he fills us with his Holy Spirit. We become his living temples.

Here on earth, he puts all things under our feet that we might rule his creation — from mere houseflies to rivers and seas, we're his stewards.

Now, that's self-esteem!

Notice how if your self-image is too low, God will bring you up a notch. If I say, "I'm bad," God reminds me that he looked on all that he had made, myself included, and he affirmed, "It's very good!" Who am I to quarrel with the Lord?

On the other hand, if I let my self-esteem get too high, God will see to it that I'm brought down a notch. Remember the king in Daniel 4:28 who went out on his porch to look over his kingdom and congratulate himself for being such a clever man to create all he saw? The Lord struck him with madness and he became as a dog that ate grass until he knew that God was the Lord.

You see, God will get you both ways! Low or high, he brings our self-esteem into balance.

Conclusion

Walking onto the beach from the boardwalk this summer, I saw a young lady who was rather obese and had a bad case of acne. She was red with sunburn and breathing heavily as she labored up the stairs. Her eyes caught mine and I saw into her soul — the loneliness, the self-loathing, the pain. I asked God, "Can a person like her ever find happiness in life?"

And the answer came. Not if she looks for her self-worth in things or people or beauty or talent or acclaim. But if she comes to know Jesus Christ, if she with the poet of Psalm 8 becomes impressed with who God is and what he has done in creation, and discovers herself to be a part of his brilliant masterpiece, she can.

And what about you? And me? We'll never have adequate self-esteem until we stand beside our majestic Lord and say, "O Lord, our Lord, how majestic is thy name in all the earth."

Suggested Prayer
O Jesus, you have made me. Cause me to love you, along with creation, self included. Amen.

---

1. Edwin Arlington Robinson, "Richard Cory," written in the early 1920s. In the public domain.

Psalm 19

Directions Included!

The law of the Lord is perfect, reviving the soul.
— Psalm 19:7a

I recently sat and talked with a woman who had a hoop with cloth stretched over it. She was embroidering. As the conversation turned to spiritual matters, she surprised me with her honesty, confessing, "I realize what's wrong with me. My life is not framed. It's loose, sloppy, without a border. I have no concept who or where I am. What I need is a frame."

Certainly, this woman's lament is no solitary cry in the dark, but part of a vast chorus of humanity crying out for meaning in life. Psalm 19 can give us that frame. It's so beautifully written. I'm reluctant to teach on it for fear of spoiling it.

Verse 14 is a famous collect. "Let the words of my mouth and the meditation of my heart be pleasing in thy sight, O Lord, my rock and my redeemer."

The whole notion of our lives being pleasing to God is foreign to us. "He should be pleasing to me! Not me to him!" Ah, but God is our creator, and we are his creatures. If I please him, then perhaps my life will become *pleasing*. Therefore, I can be happily fulfilled.

But how? How can one live to please the Lord? What direction do we take? Psalm 19 explains we're not on our own to find a pleasing life. God is here to help us along the path.

God Gives Information

Psalm 19 begins by declaring that God is not silent. He speaks and he shares truth — information about himself, ourselves, life, and the direction. Imagine David, a lonely shepherd boy out under the stars on a hillside. The vast Milky Way is spreading above him and he writes, "The heavens declare the glory of God, and the sky above proclaims his handiwork. Day to day pours forth speech and night to night reveals knowledge." Hear those key words — declare, proclaim, speech, knowledge — all this is "poured" out upon us night and day?

When my son was eight, he bought a GI Joe aircraft carrier with over 2,000 parts. The box said, "Some assembly required." We opened it in his room and spread the parts out on the floor. The directions were written in Chinese and translated into a baffling English mish mash. We quickly became frustrated trying to make sense of it all.

How like life! So many parts! Such complexity! So much confusion! Where do I get information? Directions? What is first? Second?

Most of us learn by trial and error. I do mean trial and I do mean error. You've seen insects that have long antennae. These bugs feel their way along. Many people also feel their way along in life. Wanting to be happy, we decide it's in feelings — money, sex, ice cream, resorts, or drugs. We wear out each experience and by a long process of elimination find out more about what happiness is not than what it is. By then we are old and cynical.

Happy living, however, comes not from feelings, but from facts. Right living starts with truth; right thinking leads to right behavior followed by good feelings.

Psalm 19 explains how God gives us truth. First, he speaks through nature.

- Creation
    The heavens declare the glory of God.
    Nature, creation, speaks of order — the sun, moon, and stars have the precision of a Swiss watch.
- Reliability
    Day to day
    Night to night
    Without fail
- Beauty
    Sunsets
    The heavens

Some of God's best sermons are out-of-doors
Spoken in nature
In stars above
- Immensity
His voice goes out to the entire world

An African missionary told me to go see Victoria Falls before I die. "After seeing such, one is never the same again." Ah, yes, the grandeur of nature!

George W. Carver, the agriculturist and peanut scientist, wrote, "I love to think of nature as an unlimited broadcasting system through which God speaks to us every hour if we will only tune Him in."

A second way God gives us truth is through the conscience. Sir Isaac Newton built a mechanical model of the solar system. One wound it up to make it move the planets in orbit around the sun. An atheist friend of Newton's saw it and explained, "My, Newton, what an exquisite thing! Who made it?" "Nobody," Newton said. But his friend would have none of it. Such design requires a designer.

And so it is that the human conscience stoutly proclaims: if there is a creation there must be a creator. This orderly, reliable, beautiful, immense universe speaks of such a God!

The third way God gives us information is through Jesus. Christ said, "If you have seen me you have seen the Father" (John 14). Verses 7-11 speak of Christ as God's law, his word, his revelation of himself.

The sweet poet of Israel tells us God's word is
- Authoritative
   The law of the Lord
   Statutes
   Precepts
   Ordinances
- Attractive
   It is like gold, honey, and brings reward (vv. 10-11)
- Abrasive
   Warned (v. 11)

Faults (v. 12)
Errors (v. 12)
Scripture is very bold in correcting us
- Active
   Jesus requires a response
   Reviving the soul (v. 7)
   Makes one wise (v. 7)
   Enlightening the eyes (v. 8)

Sir Walter Scott summed this up well in his "Tribute to the Bible."

> *Within this awful volume lies*
> *The mystery of mysteries:*
> *Happiest they of human race,*
> *To whom their God has given grace*
> *To read, to fear, to hope, to pray*
> *To lift the latch, to force the way;*
> *But better had they ne'er been born*
> *Who read to doubt or read to scorn.*[1]

God Gives Motivation

God gives us information and the Lord also gives inspiration. He gives motivation.

In Psalm 19, the poet theologue uses the sun as an illustration of God's motivating light. The sun "comes forth like a bridegroom leaving his tent" (v. 5). He "runs his course with joy." "Nothing is hid from his heat."

Today we can even add to this! The sun is 93 million miles away. It is so large, a million earths could abide in its girth and its light travels at 186 million miles per second — so what?

The power from sunlight has been rated at hundreds of horsepower per square foot — so what?

The hot sun can motivate you to put on your swimsuit and go for a dip to cool off. It can burn you, inspiring one to wearing tanning lotion. It can even move you to seek shade.

Psalm 19 says God's word impacts us by creation, conscience, and Christ — so what? God's word is like the sun. Nothing is hidden from its heat. It runs its course around the globe. And Christ is like a bridegroom seeking a people to be his bride — so what? Information alone is not enough. The twenty-first-century western church is awash in information — books, tapes, radio, television, small groups. and counseling. We know the facts — so what?

- Swimming is the best exercise.
- Chocolate is fattening.
- I shouldn't watch movies like this.
- Tithing brings blessing.
- Going to class is important.

We know it. What we lack is motivation.

My eight-year-old son liked to start his weekends on Friday mornings. He'd feign an illness and beg to sleep in. So I motivated him. "Son, stay in bed. The doctor will come. He'll give you a shot. And his needle is this big!" He was up, dressed, and out the door in no time!

We, too, need motivation to be inspired, to be needled! The text gives us clues in our longing to know God, to live a happy meaningful life....

Verse 9 tells us, "the fear of the Lord" motivates us. That is "awe," the "reverence" we have for God.

Verse 11 explains, "In keeping them is great reward." A blessing, happiness, comes in obedience.

Verse 14 mentions what is "pleasing in thy sight." I want to please God. I love him. I don't want God on my case!

Verse 8 speaks of God's precepts, "rejoicing the heart." Joy and happiness are by-products of a life conducted in God's will. It speaks of a clear commandment "enlightening the eyes." I seek to be wise and intelligent.

God Gives Integration

God, in the complexity of life, gives us information and motivation. He also gives integration. In verse 14, the poet asks in prayer that "The words of my mouth and the mediations of my heart be acceptable." He is praying he can receive God's information, apply it in thought and deed so that God will be his "rock and redeemer, his foundation and Savior."

You see faith is a thorough matter. It must all fit together. As the hot sun impacts us and causes us to change out of our woolens and into a bathing suit, so God's information gets into our thinking, motivates our behavior, and leads us to live a life pleasing to him.

God is our *rock*, on him we build our way of marriage, our finances, our labor, our speech, and our mercy. It's all integrated in him, a rich fabric of truth.

C. S. Lewis was an early author and mentor of mine. While a student in England, in 1971, I visited Oxford University where he once taught. At Magdalen College, I asked a janitor if he knew Dr. Lewis. "Why, yes," he said with pleasure. "Dr. Lewis was the most thoroughly converted Christian I ever knew."

You see, ours is not a shallow life. Information does not come in one ear and go out the other. God informs us. He motivates us. We integrate our lives in him.

Conclusion

A teenager recently told me, "I belong to the blank generation. I have no beliefs. I belong to no community, no tradition, or anything like that. I'm lost in this vast world. I belong nowhere I have absolutely no identity." Back to the lady embroidering cloth on an oval frame. Our life requires such a frame, as well. Here it is in Jesus Christ! Stretch your life around him!

Suggested Prayer
O Lord, take me to yourself! In Christ. Amen.

---

1. Sir Walter Scott, "Tribute To The Bible," *The Monastery*, Vol. 1, Chapter XII, 1820. In the public domain.

Psalm 23:1-3

Intensive Care — Part One

The Lord is my shepherd, I shall not want; he makes me lie down in green pastures. He leads me beside still waters; he restores my soul. He leads me in paths of righteousness for his name's sake. — Psalm 23:1-3

Just this past year I visited a friend in the intensive care unit of a hospital. A heart attack had landed him there and now he was hooked up to a maze of tubes, wires, and monitors. A nurse checked in on him every ten minutes. It looked like all of modern medical know-how was committed to his health. Driving home that day, I began to muse over the great care my loved one was receiving. I began to think about how much God loves us and how he does not just provide his children with casual concern but with intensive care. And that's when I thought of Psalm 23. It is nothing but a testimony to the Lord's intensive care for his people.

We are going to be taking a look at Psalm 23 in two parts. I am going to break it apart thought by thought and see what life under God's intensive care is like.

Who Is Your Shepherd?

The psalm begins with a simple five word statement, "The Lord is my shepherd." It is David's way of acknowledging God's control of his life. It's like saying, "The Lord is my manager."

Did you know that sheep can't take care of themselves? A fox can. So can a hawk, a deer, and to a certain extent, cows, dogs, horses, and cats. But a sheep is a rather helpless animal. He is shortsighted, prone to eat poisonous plants, extremely vulnerable to predators, defenseless, and even given to depression. All this, and he tastes good! No other livestock in the world requires such diligent care as sheep. Shepherdless, a sheep would likely be dead inside a week's time.

Not only do sheep require a shepherd, but people do, too! It's rather obvious that people need leadership. We, too, are shortsighted, given to depression, vulnerable, and prone to stray. David knew these things about himself. He didn't even pretend to be able to take care of himself. That's why he made a decision to accept the Lord as his shepherd.

Be clear here! Psalm 23 gives a high view of God — compassionate shepherd, but a low view of humanity — sheep-like and needy. This is different than pop culture that says God is irrelevant and I can be impressed with myself!

What about you? Is the Lord your shepherd? Have you owned up to the fact that you can't take care of yourself? Many of you have accountants to handle your finances. Movie stars have managers, authors have their agents, and athletes their trainers. But what about your whole life? Who is your shepherd?

In Charlotte, North Carolina, there is a wealthy businessman who never makes a decision without first consulting a medium. A famous comedian uses an astrologer to order his life. And for many, Hollywood's newest star is the guide to the good life. The world is packed full of people, causes, and philosophies all seeking to be your guide, your manager, your shepherd. On you is placed the awesome responsibility of choice. You alone must choose whom you will follow.

As Christians we say, "The Lord is my shepherd," but I wonder if we mean it. I know a lot of you can quote Psalm 23, but can you mean it? What we too often mean is that the Lord is our Savior, but not our shepherd. We don't follow him. We want no part of his flock. In short, we don't act like his sheep.

What about it? Is the Lord your shepherd?

No Wants

From a simple declarative statement, "The Lord is my shepherd," the psalm moves on. It begins to discuss the consequences of a person's sheep-shepherd relationship with God. This shouldn't surprise us. Everything we do or fail to do in this world has consequences. And most certainly the guide we choose to obey will lead us into consequences. The question is, what kind?

The psalmist begins his list of consequences by saying, "I shall not want." Here he testifies that there is contentment with the Lord.

If you study the life of David, this psalm's author, you will discover that there were times when he knew great deprivation. Saul sought to kill him. His own son, Absalom, sought to overthrow the government and almost succeeded. David knew hunger and he experienced the death of several of his own children. He even knew the bitterness of marital strife and the agony of lost dreams. God forbade David to build the temple. With all this in mind, it would seem a glossy overstatement for David to write, "I shall not want."

Yet David is talking about something far deeper than the pleasure of a full stomach and money in the bank. He is talking about contentment. You know that many rich people are restless malcontents, while so many poor or modest folks are serene. The truth is that contentment doesn't come with things or money or power. It comes from God.

Do you know God in such a way that you are in a state of contentment? Some years ago, a young lady was found dead behind a laundromat in California. She died of a drug overdose. The coroner found this note on her body. It was a testimony to her shepherd.

King Heroin is my shepherd.
I shall not want.
He maketh me to lie down in filthy gutters.
He leadeth me in the paths of crime for the sake of a
 fix.
Yea, though I walk through the valley of the shadow of
 death,
I will fear, fear, fear all evil for thou art with me.
Thy needle and thy fix, they try to comfort me.
Thou robbest the groceries from the table in front of my
 family.
Our cups are dry.

> *Surely fear and pain shall follow me all the days of my life,*
> *And I shall dwell in the house of torment and hell forever.*
> — Author unknown

David's testimony is in stark contrast with this lady's. David said his shepherd was the Lord. She said hers was drugs. David said, "I shall not want." She said she was always in need of a "fix." What about you? Is God your manager? Are you content?

Green Fields

David points out a further consequence of his relationship with God. He says, "He makes me to lie down in green pastures." To understand this comment one has to know sheep. Grass is their main diet. And where are they resting? "In green pastures." The shepherd doesn't lead his flock to barren, stony fields. He leads them to lush, green pastures where their hunger is best satisfied.

It is also interesting to note that sheep have been known to overindulge themselves. Starting out at four in the morning, sheep eat constantly. They are never still. They walk continuously as they graze. By ten in the morning, the sun is blazing in the sky and the sheep are hot, tired, and thirsty. Yet, the good shepherd knows that if his sheep drink water on top of a full stomach of undigested grass they will become ill. So he makes them to lie down in the soft grass. Since sheep will not eat while lying down, they begin to ruminate and digest what they have consumed.

Those of you who've had children know how this is. Children don't know how to do anything in moderation. They play at full throttle. They want to eat all the candy in their Easter baskets in one day. And a child nearing the point of exhaustion will never even consider taking a nap. That's why a parent must make them stop playing and eating candy and lie down to rest. As adults, we somehow never quite outgrow some of our childish ways. An overly busy minister in our area was recently struck down with back pains and had to be hospitalized. A fellow minister came to see him and said, "Charles, I've just one thing to say to you — he makes me to lie down!"

Like sheep and children, sometimes we just do not know when to stop. We overindulge in everything from food and alcohol to work. We spend our money as if there were no tomorrow. We're always in a hurry! We live at such a frantic pace that we take no time to lie down on green pastures and digest life. How long has it been since you sat on the front porch in a rocking chair? What happened to naps, long walks with the family, and hammocks in the shade? In our quest for money, fame, success, and pleasure, we have forgotten how to lie down, to be still and meditate, and to digest life. We need a heavenly Father who will stop us like children and make us take a nap. We need a shepherd who will make us to lie down in green pastures for our own good.

Still Waters

David says of God, "He leads me beside still waters." This doesn't mean "distilled water" like I used to think as a child. It means calm waters, a quiet pool from which to drink. Sheep are afraid of water. If their thick coats of wool get wet while they drink in a stream they could be pulled under and drowned. So, built into each sheep is an instinctive fear of swiftly moving streams. The shepherd knows this and takes them only to quiet pools of "still water."

Also of note is the fact that the text says, "He leads me" to the water. Sheep don't select their own watering holes. The shepherd does. That's because sheep aren't very choosy about where they drink just so long as the water is still. They'll lap water out of a hoof print filled with filthy water. They'll even sip from a stagnant pool. And the results can be devastating! Dirty water can contain liver flukes, nematodes, and parasites that ultimately riddle a sheep with disease. So the shepherd selects the drinking spots, not the sheep, and it is always a quiet pool of pure water.

Now, of what consequence is it to you and me to be led by still waters today? Just this: We, like sheep, can get in over our heads and drown. We too can drink innocently from some scummy water hole and become infested with religious diseases like astrology, gurus, Transcendental Meditation, Jehovah's Witnesses, and other cults. Just like sheep, we need to be led by God.

Perhaps there is another point here that is sometimes hidden from us. Not many of you know it, but sheep can go for days, even months, without actually taking a drink of water. That's because the grass they eat early in the morning has dew on it, and it provides for their moisture requirements. So "still water" can mean "dew." "He leads me to the early morning dew," the text says. Shepherds usually begin feeding their flock early in the morning while the dew is on the ground. They do this especially in areas where water is scarce. The still water, the dew, slakes the thirst of the lambs.

God, our shepherd, would have us rise early and feed on him, as well. Remember the gospel song, "In The Garden"? Its words say, "I come to the garden alone, while the dew is still on the roses ... and he walks with me and he talks with me...." A study of the lives of the great saints will point out that they rose early while the dew was still on the ground. And early they communed with God in their devotions. This was their still water that quenched their thirst throughout the day. We, too, can lick that same dew and be satisfied.

And you? Does your shepherd make you content? Does he lead you to green grass and quiet pools of pure water?

Restoration

A further point David makes about his shepherd is restoration. "He restores my soul," the text says. Now the question might immediately arise, "If the Lord is such a good shepherd why then do his sheep need restoration?" Simply this: life takes its toll on us all in wear and tear simply in the living. And then there are our constant strayings. This is no reflection on the shepherd's ability to lead. It is a reflection on our ability to follow.

Have you ever heard of a cast-down sheep? It is a phrase used for a sheep that has rolled over on his back and can't right himself. That's right! Sheep are just like turtles. Once they are on their backs they can't get up without help. You can believe that wolves and vultures like to find cast-down sheep! They make an easy meal!

It is the shepherd's job to count his flock daily to see if any are missing and if all are on their feet. When the shepherd discovers a cast-down sheep, he tenderly rolls him over and helps him regain his footing. No shepherd would kick his sheep when they're down. "He restores their soul."

We can become cast down and helpless, too, can't we? King David strayed off into an adulterous affair with Bathsheba. He got tangled up in a sex scandal that ultimately led to murder, judgment, and anarchy. It took God to get him on his feet again. Look at Psalm 42:11. David wrote, "Why are you *cast down*, O my soul, and why are you disquieted within me? Hope in God; For I shall again praise him, my help and my God."

This is a great promise from God. When we stray, he will right us. When life puts us on our back in helplessness, the shepherd comes. He restores our soul. With God there is always the hope of regaining our footing.

He Leads Me

In the final portion of our text for today David says, "He leads me in the paths of righteousness for his name's sake." Notice it doesn't say, "He pushes me" or "He drives me." It says, "He leads me." Shepherds lead their sheep from the front.

Isn't this just how the Lord leads us? He leads by going on ahead. We simply follow in his steps. He has led us by example, by ministry, by love, by forgiveness. He has gone on ahead to suffer and die and rise again — and we follow.

Of particular note in this part of the text is the fact that sheep are shortsighted. They cannot see five feet in front of them. Hence a sheep can easily stray and fall off a cliff or get into deep water. This is why the shepherd leads his flock by maintaining close contact with his sheep. He leads them in the right paths, the paths that lead to the green pastures and the still waters.

God leads us in the right paths like this, too. He keeps in close contact with us through the Holy Spirit, prayer, scripture, the sacraments, and worship. He knows we cannot see far and are likely to wander off on some wrong path, so he stays close. This is for a reason. The text says it's for "his name's sake." A scraggly, sick, and undernourished flock that regularly loses one or two sheep to wolves advertises a bad shepherd. But a well-fed flock that is content and ruminating in green pastures is an indication of the presence of a good shepherd. So it is for the sake of God's own good name that he cares for the sheep he calls his own. We are advertisements for his intensive care.

Here's how it works in our neighborhood: You choose Jesus as your shepherd and as you follow him, the consequences begin to pile up in your life. You seem content. Good character and restoration are with you. Your friends, who may be following other shepherds, see and wonder why you have it so good when they don't. It's a witness! And it is for the Lord's namesake that he uses you to lead others into his flock.

All I Want!

In a Sunday school class, I asked a six-year-old girl if she knew Psalm 23. "Yes, I do!" She beamed with pride. "Will you say it for me?" I inquired. She agreed and said rather matter-of-factly, "The Lord's my shepherd. That's all I want!" From the mouths of babes! But, how about you? Is the Lord your shepherd? Does he manage your life? Is his guidance all you want?

Suggested Prayer

Lord, I want you for more than a Savior. I want you for my shepherd, as well. Make me as one of your sheep. For Christ's sake. Amen.

Psalm 23:4-6

Intensive Care — Part Two

Even though I walk through the valley of the shadow of death, I fear no evil; for thou art with me; thy rod and thy staff, they comfort me. Thou preparest a table before me in the presence of my enemies; thou anointest my head with oil, my cup overflows. Surely goodness and mercy shall follow me all the days of my life; and I shall dwell in the house of the Lord for ever.
— Psalm 23:4-6

It will help you to understand Psalm 23 if you can imagine two sheep, one on either side of a fence. The sheep on the right is well-fed, healthy, and at peace. The sheep on the left is scraggly, hungry, and tormented. The healthy sheep is boasting through the fence to the less-fortunate sheep about the benefits of his shepherd. "Why do you have it so good?" the scraggly sheep asks. The healthy animal answers, "The Lord is my shepherd, I shall not want; he makes me lie down in green pastures. He leads me beside still waters; he restores my soul. he leads me in the paths of righteousness for his name's sake" (Psalm 23:1-3).

Now we are at the halfway point in this poem. The sheep now stops addressing his psalm to other sheep and begins talking to the shepherd himself. And he talks about all the good things the shepherd does for him.

Companionship

The psalm first mentions the shepherd's companionship. "Even though I walk through the valley of the shadow of death, I fear no evil; for thou art with me." Sheep are timid little creatures. They jump at strange sounds and balk at unknown experiences. When the grass is depleted on the lower slopes and the shepherd leads them to higher ground where the grass is, sometimes it's necessary to take some difficult and unknown trails that lead through shadowy canyons. Quite naturally the sheep fear such pathways and it's only the familiar voice of the shepherd that emboldens them to go on.

I have a minister friend named John who is afraid of flying. He recently held a meeting in New Orleans and had to fly home. When John arrived at the airport, there was fog everywhere. You couldn't even see the tip of the airplane wing! My friend's pulse quickened with fear as he buckled his seatbelt. Then the door to the cockpit opened and out strode the captain who turned out to be a member of John's former church in Philadelphia. The captain put the minister at ease. All through the flight, John kept saying to himself, "Captain Jameson loves me. He's with me. He won't let anything happen to me!" God is with us like that, too. He has been born among us. Even his name is Emmanuel, which means, "God is with us." The Lord is at the controls of the universe. He loves us. He will see us, not to, but *through* the valley of the shadows.

The Shepherd's Tools

Next, the sheep begins to talk about the shepherd's tools. He mentions a rod and a staff and says, "They comfort me."

The shepherd's rod was a short, hard stick that was carried to protect the flock. It could be used to crush a snake or break the back of a coyote. You can believe that to a defenseless sheep the rod was a comfort.

God protects us with his own hand, as well. It was the Lord who broke Satan's power on Calvary. It was the Lord who smote Egypt with the plagues, saying, "Let my people go." And it is the Lord who gives his angels charge of us, still.

This part of the text also mentions the shepherd's staff. It, too, is mentioned as being of comfort to the flock. The staff is not so much a weapon as it is a tool of discipline. While the rod was to protect the sheep from predators, the staff was to protect the sheep from themselves.

Sheep are notorious wanderers. They easily slip off the beaten path and fall into pits, into mud holes, pools, and over cliffs. The staff, a long stick with a crook on the end, is used to retrieve the wayward animal. Just hook the staff around a lamb and he is easily pulled from danger. I might add that good shepherds have also been known to use the staff to prod sheep into line, to quicken their pace, or to make them lie down.

Do you see how this fits for us today? We go astray. We get into messes that we cannot get out of — and it is the Lord who disciplines us for our own good. He might use the Holy Spirit to prod our consciences into repentance. He can use a session or a minister or some brother or sister to snatch us from harm's way.

Thank God for the shepherd's tools. They protect us from others, they protect us from ourselves, and they do comfort us.

A Prepared Table

Passing on from the tools of the shepherd's trade, we come to this verse: "Thou preparest a table before me in the presence of my enemies."

A few years ago, I was doing a funeral and the family requested me not to read Psalm 23. "She didn't have any enemies," they explained. Well, this part of the text does not mean that God lets us feast while our enemies stand around the table and drool. It means that the shepherd decides what his flock shall eat.

Sheep are not choosy about what they nibble. They'll sample a poisonous weed, grow ill, and die. They have little sense of what's good for them. So it is that the shepherd goes into the fields before his sheep arrive. He carefully uproots and burns all poisonous weeds, nettles, and the like. Thus he prepares the table before his sheep.

God will do the same thing for us if we'll let him. Like sheep, some Christians feel like they have to try everything that comes their way. Some people fall for every religious fad that comes along; indulge themselves to their own harm. But God would prepare our diet for us. The Ten Commandments are given not to restrict us but to keep us from harm. When the Bible warns us to keep our minds pure from idolatry, astrology, hate, and the like, it's not stripping the "goodies" from the table. It's warning us against poison. There are enemies to the faith. There are poisons in the world and unless we are willing to let God prepare our diet, we're going to eventually get into trouble.

How about you? Will you let God prepare a table for you in the presence of your enemies?

Oil

"Thou anointest my head with oil," the sheep says. He is speaking of an oil made up of linseed, sulfur, and tar that the shepherd poured over his sheep in the spring and summer. You well know what pests deer flies, nasal flies, and mosquitoes can be. Such pests cause sheep no end of torment. They can drive a flock into a frenzy, causing blindness and inflammation. Sheep have even been known to bash their heads against rocks to ease the torment. That's why the good shepherd puts oil on the head of his sheep. It is a bug repellent. It's the equivalent of the modern-day flea collar.

What's bugging you today? Are there frustrations and personality conflicts that buzz about you waiting for a chance to sting you, to take your blood? How much does your work suffer, how ineffective have you become due to worry over some pesky problem? When the Panama Canal was being dug, mosquitoes all but halted the project. Only when an effective means of controlling this pest was developed was work able to continue. What about you? Has God anointed your head with oil so that you can go about your business in a relaxed and effective way?

A Japanese Christian businessman wrote his version of this psalm. Listen to it and see if he doesn't have an anointing of oil.

> *The Lord is my pacesetter,*
> *I shall not rush.*
> *He makes me stop for quiet intervals.*
> *He provides me with images of stillness*
> *which restore my serenity.*
> *He leads me in ways of efficiency*
> *through calmness of mind,*
> *and his guidance is peace.*
> *Even though I have a great many things*
> *to accomplish each day,*
> *I will not fret,*

for his presence is here.
His timelessness, his all-importance,
will keep me in balance.
He prepares refreshment and reward
and renewal in the midst of my activity
by anointing my mind with his oil and tranquility.
My cup of joyous energy overflows.
Surely harmony and effectiveness shall be the fruit of
my hours,
And I shall walk in the peace of the Lord
and dwell in his house forever.[1]

The Overflowing Cup

Still talking to the shepherd, the sheep now says rather ecstatically, "My cup overflows." Here the sheep is simply remembering how his keeper even provides something to drink when water is unavailable. When sheep can't get to water, the shepherd brings water to the sheep. Sometimes the shepherd even mixes a bit of medicine in the water when his flock is in need. Each lamb is given an overflowing draught.

Perhaps a lady in Charlotte County, Virginia, best summed up this part of the text for us when she said, "Da Lawd done filled my cup and slopped it over into da saucer, too!" Certainly, God is not stingy with his people. He fills our cups to overflowing. If you've ever seen a football game you know how this is. The team calls for time out and the coach sends out the bucket of Gatorade. Each player is given an overflowing cupful to quench his thirst and restore his salt needs.

T. S. Eliot once wrote, "We measure our lives by the spoonful when our cups overflow." Isn't it the truth? We only count a small percentage of our blessings. We pray like God is stingy. Our cups overflow but we don't notice. Didn't Jesus make the wine to overflow at a wedding banquet? Didn't he provide bread and fish at a picnic so that more than 5,000 could eat? And will not our heavenly Father lavish his blessings on us still?

Pursued!

The psalmist begins to sum up the consequences of his shepherd-sheep relationship with God now. He says confidently, "Surely goodness and mercy shall follow me all the days of my life."

There are some who have tried to say that "goodness" and "mercy" are sheep dogs that, like angels, watch the flock. Though this is a stretch of the text it is true that angels watch over us. The real key to this part of the text is the phrase "shall follow me." A literal Hebrew translation is "shall pursue me." "Surely goodness and mercy shall *pursue* me all the days of my life." You've been chased by a dog or a bull or a lover or a police car, no doubt. But have you ever been chased by goodness and mercy?

King David had been chased by Saul, by murderous Philistines, pestilences. and even the giant, Goliath. But, most of all, he says it's God's goodness and mercy that follow him, yes, that *pursue* him all the days of his life.

Stop and think here for a moment. Isn't this true for you as a Christian? God is pursuing you. What will he do if he catches you? He'll bless you! In most worship services God promises to bless you and keep you, to make his face to shine upon you and give you peace (Numbers 6:22-27). With such a blessing pursuing us all the days of our lives, I'm not going to be too hard for God to catch. Is it any wonder the psalmist ends his poem as he does?

I'm Staying Put

He says, "And I shall dwell in the house of the Lord forever." Here the psalmist makes a willful decision to remain in God's flock forever. It's as if he knows a good thing when he sees it!

A *Peanuts* cartoon strip shows Lucy telling Charlie Brown, "I think it's so important for a day to start off right, don't you, Charlie?" Little Charlie sheepishly says, "I think it's more important that it end right." And certainly this psalm starts and ends right. It begins with an affirmation, "The Lord is my shepherd." It ends as the sheep says, "I'll dwell in the Lord's house all the time." That's like a soldier saying, "This is the best outfit in the Army. I'll never leave this group!" And so it is that David plans to live as God's sheep forevermore.

Do You Know The Shepherd?

What can I say in summing up such a psalm? What is the effect such a psalm will have on you?

At a large university some years ago, a rather famous poet came to read his poetry. After the reading, a woman asked if he'd read Psalm 23. He agreed, and with flawless execution he rendered the psalm. The crowd was impressed. They clapped their hands in praise.

Yet another request came from the crowd. Someone asked that a local, retired pastor who was in attendance read the psalm, also. With a voice cracking with age and colored with country twang, the old pastor falteringly read Psalm 23. This time the people wept.

Stepping to the microphone the poet commented on the crowd's response. "I see what the difference is," he said. "I know the psalm, but he knows the shepherd."

You who know this psalm from memory, do you know the shepherd? Have you made a willful decision to be a sheep in his flock? Perhaps you've been following other flocks, obeying the call of other shepherds and today you feel it hasn't worked out so well. The consequences were terrible. Maybe you'd like to change shepherds. The choice is up to you. The door to God's flock is open. Come on in if you will.

Suggested Prayer

Lord, open the door, I'm coming in! Make me one of your own sheep. For Christ's sake. Amen.

---

1. http://www.fcchurch.com/templates/cusfee/details.asp?i.

Psalm 27

At Peace In A Fearful World

The Lord is my light and my salvation; whom shall I fear? The Lord is the stronghold of my life; of whom should I be afraid? — Psalm 27:1

Two hoboes walk up to the gate of a farmhouse. A dog is there growling, his teeth bared and his tail wagging! One man pauses. The other chides, "Go on! Knock on the door and ask for lunch." To which the hobo retorts, "I don't know which end of the dog to believe!"

Ah, the debilitating nature of fear....

Psalm 27 mentions fear three times. He laments "... whom shall I fear? ... of whom shall I be afraid?" (v. 1); "evildoers assail me" (v. 2), "a host encamp against me" (v. 3), "the day of trouble" (v. 5), and "Give me not up to the will of my adversaries" (v. 12).

See the fear, the anxiety, and the worry swirling as a storm around the psalmist?

The number one health problem of women is anxiety. With men it is alcoholism, with fear being second.

The top five fears are being alone, rejection, cancer, death, and failure. And unless one masters fear, it will surely master you! In fact, to be happy one must somehow defeat fear in one's life. And here is where Psalm 27 can be helpful.

Causes Of Fear

Fear can come from *environmental causes*. In Psalm 27, David lives in a war zone. There are enemies who imperil his throne ... the Philistines and disloyal aides; even Absalom, his own son.

Today, our homes or our marriages can be a combat zone. In verse 10, David wails that "my mother and father have forsaken me." Sometimes we grow up with learned anxieties. Broken homes scar us.

Two really big phobias are

- Fear of failure — "When I lost a sporting event, my father yelled for days."
- Fear of rejection — "If I disappointed my father he wouldn't speak to me for two weeks."

Fear can come from *temperamental causes*. It's clear David had a melancholy temperament. Sensitive, evaluative, an eye for detail, loyal. This was David, the sweet psalmist of Israel. The fact is some people are more prone to fear than others.

Then there are *psychological causes* of anxiety. For instance, David's war traumas with the Philistines or his stressful single combat with Goliath.

Finally, some phobias come from *spiritual causes* — lack of faith, sin, and disobedience. When Adam and Eve sinned, they hid from God in fear (Genesis 3:18). David coveted Bathsheba, killed her husband, and tried to live like nothing was wrong. All the while he feared God's judgment would catch up with him.

Characteristics Of Fear

In the story of David's life, one can see his fear that past sins will catch up to him. He was afraid of civil war, of anarchy, and he was afraid his rebel son, Absalom, would be butchered.

A good picture of fear is the Old Testament patriarch, Jacob. A slippery fellow, the quintessential con man, if you shook his hand you'd want to count your fingers!

Jacob talked his hungry brother into selling his birthright for a pot of soup. Then he stole his blessing by tricking his blind father, and he left town in a hurry.

In the countryside he ran into Laban and these two richly deserved each other. They each met their match as they proceeded to swindle one another!

Years later, Jacob wanted to go home, but he was afraid. Behind him was Laban, angry and swindled. Before him was Esau and the unknown. Jacob was sandwiched between his guilty past, a foreboding future, and an inadequate present.

Left alone, at night, Jacob started to think. Oh, the shame! Oh, the fears! There is never enough parties, enough beer, enough escapist trips, and enough lucrative business deals to solace such a life. What was he afraid of?

- The past — "What have I done?"
- The future — "What'll happen to me?"
- The present — "There's nothing I can do!"

Cure Of Fear

So, fear has many causes: environmental, temperamental, psychological, and even spiritual. Fear can lodge in our past, in our present, and in our future.

The cure of fear begins with *conviction*. Look closely at verses 5-6. David is singing his conviction. Convictions about his future! "The Lord is my light and my salvation." He calls God his stronghold, his sword, his shield. In other words, "As I go forward these go with me."

Rudyard Kipling wrote, "Of all the liars in the world, sometimes the worst are your fears."

A recent study of fears of the future found that 40% of them never happen, 30% of them happen but don't matter, 12% happen but you can handle them and 18% happen but in some better way than you imagined them.

In other words, God's light, sword, and shield are at work in our lives. Romans 8:28 promises, "We know that in everything God works for good." An amazing verse! What it does to our fear!

Then there are *convictions about our past*. Galatians 6:7 warns, "What you sow you reap." For example, David was lawless with Bathsheba. His own son, Absalom, followed years later becoming a rebel.

Our guilty past rears its ugly head. We ask, "Will this catch up with me?" "Will I pay?" "Will I be embarrassed?" Davis flees to God. In verse 1, he soothes, "The Lord is my salvation." He saves us, forgiving us of all our past transgressions.

Finally there is *conviction about the future.*

- "Will I be adequate?"
- "Will I stumble in my job interview?"
- "What do I say when I confront my child?"
- "I'm pregnant with an immoral past. What do I do?"

God promises, "As thy days so shall thy strength be." (Deuteronomy 33:25).

His shield, his light, and his sword go with us. Corrie ten Boom said it well, "Never be afraid to trust an unknown future to a known God."

This is David's conviction for past, present, and future. My relationship with Jesus fits at every point!

Another step toward release from fear is in *conquest.* David recognizes his enemy: "Evil men come up against me." He relates his problem to God. "I'm scared. I see my enemy, but I also see God and he is greater than my enemy." In this strength David resists the temptation to run. Rather, he stays to face matters. See in the psalm how David's enemy runs and stumbles while David is confident? He sings his worship. His life is high, set upon a rock.

To put matters simply: Do the thing you fear and the death of your fears is certain.

Conviction of God in your past, present, and future. *Conquest* of fear is by facing things, relating it to God, and fighting. Now, *confidence*: "though an army besiege me ... I will see goodness!"

As we live the Christian life, we gain momentum, a sense of confidence in Christ. This is like the man who wanted to be buried in his Ford truck. "I never been in a hole yet it ain't got me out of." Likewise, and more so in Jesus Christ! He's never failed me yet!

Finally, there is *consistency.* David's fears popped up. But David consistently handled every one with faith.

- "One thing have I asked of the Lord. That will I seek after" (v. 4).
- "I will offer sacrifices in his tent with shouts of joy" (v. 6).

- "Teach me thy way, O Lord; and lead me on a level path" (v. 11)
- "Wait for the Lord and be strong" (v. 14).

Adlai Stevenson said it well: "Patriotism is not a short, frenzied outburst of emotion, but the tranquil and steady dedication of a lifetime." Such is faithfulness — the steady plodding of a life hidden in Christ's light, shield, and sword.

Conclusion

The most often repeated command in scripture is "Fear not." The most oft repeated promise is, "I am with thee."

You find it 365 times, once for every day of the year.

You see, there is a sword of God, a shield, a light, a fortress of Christ encompassing you, enfolding your past, your present, and future.

Fear not.

Suggested Prayer
Lord, I hide myself in thee. Amen.

Psalm 32

Am I *That* Forgiven?

> *I acknowledged my sin to thee, and I did not hide my iniquity; I said, "I will confess my transgressions to the Lord"; then thou didst forgive the guilt of my sin.*
> — Psalm 32:5

The first word in Psalm 32 is "blessed." It means "happy." "Happy are those whose transgression is forgiven."

This was Augustine's favorite psalm. Saint Augustine was a fifth-century playboy — a drunk, cynic, father of an illegitimate child, and a North African from today's Algiers. He was converted to Christ, and later became a bishop of the church. Some fancy him to be Christianity's greatest writer and apologist.

When dying, Augustine had this psalm written on the wall by his bed so he could read it constantly.

Let's read it now and see what light there is for the living of our days.

Instruction

In the psalm there are the words "transgression," "sin," "iniquity," and "deceit." The root word for sin is found in Judges 20:16, a verse describing men so good with a slingshot they could "sling a stone at a rabbit and not miss." Sin means to miss the mark, to fall short. One can hear the same idea in Romans 3:23, "All have sinned and *fallen short* of the glory of God." In other words, none of us has hit the bull's-eye for which God has created us.

This is the story of Genesis 1-3, the opening pages of scripture. Adam and Eve were created by God, in his image, with a healthy body, spirit, and soul. They were judged good, but in turning from God by Satan's temptation, they fell short into a lifestyle of disbelief, disobedience, fear, avoidance, and lying.

Each day the news informs me of yet another American soldier killed in Iraq. The media goes on to herald the details of a car bomb in some Baghdad market that killed or maimed 170 people.

"How," I ask, "can people do that to one another? Such butchers!" Then I remember reading about July 30, 1864, Petersburg, Virginia. Yankee troops from Burnsides' corps, Pennsylvanians mostly, tunneled under Confederate lines, laid in a huge gunpowder supply, and detonated it in early dawn. Several hundred South Carolinians of Pegram's brigade were killed in the blast. A gap was blown in the rebel lines, and a Negro division of federal troops was sent into the breach. The rebels recovered, badly mauling the northern troops. The casualties were 5,300 men.

In retaliation for the Battle of the Crater, two rebels put a time bomb on a federal ammunition ship anchored among hundreds of other vessels in the Appomattox River, Virginia. The explosion destroyed at least fourteen ships and killed or maimed an unknown number of people. Most bodies were unrecognizable.

As the French say, "The more things change, the more they stay the same."

George Bernard Shaw wrote, "There is only one empirically verifiable doctrine of theology — original sin."

Look around you — everywhere we have fallen short.

- Sex — lust
- Parenting — abortion
- Foreign policy — injustice
- Marriage — divorce
- The environment — pollution

I was counseling a couple's marriage a few years ago. They quarreled in my study, and the man cursed his wife. She left in tears. He said to me, "Boy, preacher, I really missed it, didn't I?"

Yes, he missed the mark. We've all missed it and sinned. The result is misery, stress, pain, and a gnawing sense of unhappiness.

But there is good news! God forgives! Verse 1 of this psalm triumphs, "Blessed is the man whose transgression is forgiven." In scripture the idea of forgiveness means "to be let loose." It is a knot untied, prison doors thrown open, and health restored.

Verse 1 goes on to say, "Sin is covered." This does not mean swept under a rug. It means done away with!

Did you hear about the child whose cat died? He buried it with its tail sticking out. Every day he'd go pull the tail to see how the cat was doing!

Our sin is not covered over like that. Micah 7:19 says God "casts my sins in the depths of the sea." Revelation 21:1 says, "And the sea shall be no more." Psalm 103:12 reminds me God removes my sin "as far away as the East from the West." And where is the East Pole? The West Pole? In fact Isaiah 43:25 says of God, "I will remember their sins no more."

This is the good news of the gospel of Jesus Christ.

Illustration

The psalmist moves on to describe his personal experience as an unforgiven, unrepentant sinner. In verses 3-5 he laments, "For when I kept silent, my bones wasted away, through my groaning all day long. For day and night your hand was heavy upon me; my strength was dried up as by the heat of summer."

When one refuses to agree with the divine assessment of his life then life itself becomes a "groan," "dry," "weary," or "waste."

Remember those neighborhood bullies of your childhood? They'd twist your arm and not let you go until you cried, "Uncle!" Sin is like that bully who will give us no relief until we confess our sins and return to God for mercy.

Richard Baxter, the Puritan minister, explained, "Man's fall came in turning from God to himself. His salvation comes in turning from self to God." This is what the poet does. In verse 5 he shares his experience of grace.

> *I acknowledged my sin to thee.*
> *I did not hide my iniquity.*
> *I said, "I will confess my transgression to the Lord."*
> *Then thou didst forgive....*

He cried, "Uncle!" He agreed God's assessment of him was correct.

World War II was fought for the unconditional surrender of Germany and Japan. Nothing less was acceptable. And it is the same with you and me and God. We are not only sinners who need to repent, we are rebels who must stack arms and bow the knee.

Encouragement

Verse 6 begins with the word, "therefore." Since sin rules our lives, since God punishes sin but forgives the penitent, "*Therefore* let everyone who is godly offer prayer to thee...."

Notice verse 6 speaks of "prayer at a time of distress," literally, "at a time of finding." This means we must pray when God can be found. You see, there is in God's providence a ripeness, a time when the fresh breeze of the Holy Spirit is blowing. It is then the sinner must seize the opportunity.

"Don't miss your time," the psalmist is saying.

Halley's Comet is a once in a lifetime phenomenon. One must see it when it's nigh. A fresh peach is a brief delight. Eat one in season. The offer of mercy in Christ is a genuine opportunity not to be taken for granted. So, don't act like you've got all the time in the world! Seize the moment!

Some years back, there was an execution on death row in North Carolina. The condemned man told the chaplain he couldn't believe. "I am too hard-hearted!" He went on, "You see, eleven years ago I sat in a church, heard the gospel, knew it was true, but put it off. Now my life is hell-bent and I don't care."

The psalmist goes on to offer more encouragement. He writes, "In the rush of great waters, they shall not reach you." This is a reference to Noah's ark and the flood of God's judgment. "Know the time!" the poet says. "There is security in it. For the flood of God's wrath against sin is surely coming."

Now verses 8-9 encourages still more. As those who've missed the mark but been given mercy, we now turn to God and desire to live for his mark, to uphold his standard. This is not cheap grace wherein we are forgiven but go on to live in sin.

A lawyer told me of a client from the Virginia hills who was on trial for stealing a horse. The attorney won his acquittal. "What's an acquittal?" the client asked. "It means you are not guilty," the lawyer explained. "Can I still keep the horse?" the client asked.

God will have none of that! In verse 8 he says to the newly forgiven, "I will instruct you and teach you in the way you should go. I will counsel you with my eye upon you." Yes, indeed, his mercy is life-changing!

Explanation

So far, this sweet psalmist of Israel has given *instruction*, *illustration* from his own life, and *encouragement*. In verses 10-11 he helps us understand the world in which we live. He explains that there are two sorts of people:

"The wicked" have "many sorrows." And the forgiven, those who "trust in the Lord" are "surrounded" by "steadfast love." In Christ they "rejoice," and "shout for joy." In other words, they are "blessed," they are happy.

Do not fail to miss the logic of this psalm:

- those who understand sin,
- those who understand repentance,
- those who know forgiveness, and
- become those who understand rejoicing.

Conclusion

Today our culture refuses to take sin seriously.

- It is not adultery, but a little trifling indiscretion.
- It is not murder, but a woman's right to choose.
- It is not gossip but a seasoned southern bit of news sharing.
- It is no longer sabbath breaking, but just another weekend.
- It is not injustice, but acting in our national interest.

It says something about our day that we so rarely use the word sinful, except to describe a really good dessert.

Psalm 32 corrects this. It calls us to take God, our sin, and repentance seriously.

Suggested Prayer
O Lord, have mercy upon me, a sinner. Amen.

Psalm 42

Blowing Away
The Clouds Of Depression

My soul thirsts for God, for the living God. When shall I come and behold the face of God?
— Psalm 42:2

The United States is the birthplace of the blues. Guitar-wielding singers like Albert Collins, John Lee Hooker, B. B. King, and Muddy Waters sing their despair. "Don't nobody love me but my mama, and she might be jivin' me!"

Actually, the oldest form of the blues is not from America, but from the Middle East. The psalms of the Old Testament were written several thousand years ago. And fully fifty, or one third, of the psalms take the form of lament.

Psalm 42 is one such blues psalm. It is a psalm of depression. Let's open ourselves to it and see what light there is for the living of our days.

What Is Depression?

In the psalm, the singer laments, "As a deer pants for the flowing streams, so my soul longs after thee, O God." This "longing" is further detailed as a sense of "thirst," being "cast down," "disquieted within."

Health experts call depression a misery that may include feeling blue, down in the dumps, grumpiness, sadness, fatigue, copelessness, and a feeling of dejection.

In Herman Melville's book, *Moby Dick*, depression is called "a damp, drizzly November in the soul." A friend of mine describes his depression as "one of those days when you get up but can't get your closet started, one of those moments when your shoelaces seem to weigh forty pounds each."

In a *Peanuts* comic strip, Lucy has hung out her "the psychiatrist is in" sign. Charlie Brown confides, "Some days I'm up, the next day I'm down." Lucy replies, "Like an emotional roller coaster?" To which Charlie Brown responds, "No." More like the bumper cars!" Most of us can relate to getting bumped around by the hurts of life.

What is depression? It's a feeling, an emotional experience of varying intensity, that may include sadness, listlessness, dejection, and hopelessness.

What Are The Symptoms?

The psalmist is very honest. In only eleven verses he describes himself as full of longing, thirst, weeping night and day, soul cast down, disquieted within, suffocating beneath the waves, feeling forgotten, mourning, and bearing about in his person a deadly wound. My! What an eloquent expression of the blues!

Health care experts give ten major symptoms of depression:

- unexplained jumpiness or anxiety;
- unusual irritability;
- sleep disturbances;
- difficulty in concentrating or remembering;
- physical pains that are hard to pin down;
- appetite loss or overeating;
- loss of interest in job, family, sex, hobby;
- a downhearted period that gets worse or just won't go away;
- frequent unexplainable crying spells; and
- a loss of self-esteem or an attitude of indifference.

If you discover three to five of these symptoms in your life at any one time, in every likelihood you're suffering depression. That's okay — it's no sin to be downhearted. Rather, it's all a portion of what Shakespeare's Hamlet called, "The slings and arrows of outrageous fortune ... that flesh is heir to."

In the Bible, some spiritual heavyweights spent time in the doldrums. Three major prophets hurt so badly they wished for death: Moses, Elijah, and Jonah — so, you're in good company!

What Causes Depression?

Many things cause depression.

Fatigue. If I run ten miles, I become physically tired. Likewise, each of us has a tank of emotional fuel. When it is spent, I may feel blue.

Certain events in life guzzle lots of emotional energy — difficult people, rapid change, family weddings and funerals, making a speech, rejection, and the like.

Take Elijah, for example. He dueled with the prophets of Baal on Mount Carmel, slew their priests, had his life threatened by wicked Queen Jezebel, and fled into the wilderness emotionally drained. "I, only I, am left ..." he lamented.

Circumstances. A friend of mine moved against her wishes to a huge city in another part of the country. Everything was strange, her network of friends was far away, and she was feeling blue. Depression in her case was circumstantial. She's using her emotional energy to deal with change.

Nutrition. Junk food diets can lead to a junky emotional life. Today's American eats in a hurry and swills down pills and alcohol. Truman Capote, in one of his last interviews, showed up depressed, haggard looking, with his speech slurred. He confessed he hadn't slept in three days, and he had quit eating. He said he was given to mixing his pills and alcohol and drinking it as a sort of cocktail — and he was blue. Little wonder!

Biological Depression. The human body is a delicate machine and sometimes it gets out of sync. The thyroid gland can act up. There is the feminine change of life. Chemistry can become unbalanced, causing mood swings.

A Bitter Spirit. Jesus said unforgivingness turns us over to torment (Matthew 18:34). One of the worst things we can do is hate. Such creates an emotional focus wherein we eat, sleep, drink, and wrestle with our hated adversary over and over until we're thoroughly sapped by it.

A Negative Attitude. I stayed on a campus after a chapel service recently. The student who hosted me was a freshman. "How do you like it so far?" I inquired. Thus began his litany of gripes — too small, boring classes, nothing to do, no cool girls, and the dining hall food is lousy. When I asked the young man where he'd rather be, he didn't know. No wonder the student was depressed! His thoughts were an anvil about his neck.

Grief. At different times in our lives, we suffer loss. A romantic breakup, job loss, a child leaves the nest, a pet dies, divorce, estrangement from a friend, a spouse passes away ... such can lead to depression.

Sin. Facing the consequences of poor choices, carnality, quenching the Spirit, a bad conscience, failure to combat the accusations of Satan, wallowing in sin — these can depress us.

If I go hiking, I like to carry a light pack. Who'd ever think of toting a forty-pound rock around in his knapsack? Yet, sin is weighty! And many of us go through life carrying huge burdens of unconfessed sin. Hebrews 12 goads us to lighten up. "Let us throw aside every weight of sin that clings so closely, and let us run with perseverance the great race of faith set before us...."

Spirit. Times of testing come our way, what theologians call "Great Dark Nights of the Soul." Job is an example. Attacked by Satan, tested by God, Job lost his fortune, his family, his health, and his reputation. In agony, he sat on an ash heap languishing.

> *Behold, I go forward and he is not there. I go backward and I cannot find him. I turn to the right and left and cannot perceive him. But he knows the way I take. And when he has tried me I shall come forth as gold!*
> — Job 23:8-10

Indeed, many saints of history have struggled through wilderness experiences — Wesley, Luther, Elijah, Jonah, J. B. Phillips, and more.

A Mixture. In the language of depression, we speak of "triggers" as events that set off depression. And many depressions are multi-barreled — they have several triggers.

For instance, at work you are hit with financial reversals and you come home grumpy. This is the last straw for your wife and she packs up and leaves you. Depression sets in. You start eating poorly, suffer insomnia, are so ashamed you avoid your friends, quit going to church, and begin to wallow in Satan's accusations. Suddenly, you find yourself buried under an avalanche of depressive causes.

What Is The Cure?

Once when I was downhearted, I took a walk in the woods with my son. I told him my troubles, of my bleak outlook, and asked what he thought I should do. "Dad," he said, "this is serious. In any case, don't do nothing!"

In the psalm, the blues singer gives us some solid advice in healing depression.

Admit it. "My soul is cast down, disquieted within," he confesses. So many of us fake it. We think the Christian life is all rainbows and mountaintops. Yet, when we're not there, we fake it. Nothing is more pathetic than watching a half-filled Christian trying to overflow.

Express yourself. Don't bottle it up. The psalmist poured out his soul, wept, prayed to God, and talked things over with people.

Many of us, when we get down, throw a pity party and we're the only one invited. We lounge on the sofa, guzzling beer, downing chips and dip by the carload, blearily watching television. "I, only I, am left. Woe is me!"

Not the psalmist! He honestly vents his feelings to God and to helpful people.

Hope. The word is used several times in the text. Hope is enjoying the things of God's tomorrow today.

Note how the psalmist is not allowing his thoughts to drift aimlessly like lint in the wind. He directs his thoughts. He gives himself an order, "Hope in God!"

"Yes, things are bad now. But not forever! I have a wonderful Savior. He's in full control. Nothing happens to me that doesn't first come by God's permissive will. If he has allowed it, it is for some good. And I will trust all this to him and wait hopefully."

Praise. This word is used twice in the psalm. It means "to ascribe worth to God."

Many ministers experience "Blue Mondays." We can get really wrung out on a Lord's day preaching. I know I sleep a little later, get feeling sorry for myself, and mope about. Then I catch myself ascribing too much worth to people and circumstances. I'm gazing at people while only glancing at God.

Physical labor and exercise. In verse 4, the singer mentions going with the throng on a long walk up to Jerusalem's temple. In physical education, we call this "recreation." Re-creation — nothing relaxes or re-creates us like yard work, horseback riding, or an art event. It's a smart person who learns what works for him.

Memory. "These things I remember" (v. 4). The psalmist breathes, thinking of the light of better days. Again, he's arresting his thoughts, taking charge, and practicing positive thinking.

Each of us has in our memory videos of the perfect day skiing, a candlelight supper (oh, so romantic), or a fishing trip. The confidence of such past days can bolster us to face the days ahead with poise.

Accepting relapses. When one first meets the lamenter of Psalm 42, he is down, but as the psalm progresses, he improves. Then suddenly, he succumbs to a relapse. In verse 7 just as he gets his head above water, another wave comes crashing over him.

I've known some victims of depression who have been healed in a moment. But most whom I know are healed by process. And it is usually three steps forward and two steps backward.

Following are some helpful insights in curing depression that go beyond the scope of this particular psalm.

- **Look to your nutrition.** The book of Leviticus is a study of nutrition. So, evidently the good Lord is concerned with our eating habits.
- **Are you practicing forgiveness?**
- **Have you come to know yourself?** What triggers your depression? What allows you emotional rest?
- **Recognize the healing therapy of service.** A woman struggling with the postpartum blues wallowed in the emotional

doldrums over her lost figure, being up all night with a sick child, and instant full-time responsibility. For two years, the blues lasted. It lifted when she and her baby started going around to rest homes ministering to the elderly, some of whom hadn't held a baby in decades.
- **There's plenty more, but neither the psalmist nor I have the expertise.** Even the best of doctors will confess depression to be mysterious.

Conclusion

Thirty million Americans suffer from depression right now — that's one in nine.

Five percent of us are struggling with a major depression at any given time; 25% of us will do so at one time in our lives.

What the psalmist is saying needs to be heard. You are not alone. Others have been there before you. There is help. God can meet you where you are and still bring a blessing to and from your life!

Winston Churchill called depression, "A black dog that follows me about." Abe Lincoln suffered from severe, debilitating bouts of depression. So did George Friedrick Handel, the composer; Vincent van Gogh, the artist; Buzz Aldrin, the astronaut; Robert E. Lee, the general; Marilyn Monroe, the actress; and the sweet psalmist from Israel.

Whoever you are, wherever you are, know that God cares. So do his people. Reach out for help and let the healing process begin!

Suggested Prayer

Lord, you know. You know! You also care. Thank you. Help me to clasp my hand in thine! For Jesus' sake. Amen.

Psalm 46; Matthew 28:16-20

The Good Now Days!

God is our refuge and strength, a very present help in trouble. — Psalm 46:1

We have a bath shower in our house, and as with most showers, it has a water pressure problem. You get in it, adjust the water to a comfortable temperature, and suddenly your wife turns on the washing machine in the basement. The shower becomes freezing as you frantically try to adjust the tap. Then, just as you get things fixed, the washer cuts off and you're scalded! Life is like that, isn't it? Just as you get settled, just as you get used to things, something changes and you're made uncomfortable. An adjustment is called for!

What does the Bible have to say about change? What is the Christian attitude toward a world that is in flux? Our two texts deal with this subject, so let us delve into them and glean their meaning.

Never Stays The Same!

The first text, Psalm 46, tells us that the earth is a place of change. People, places, and things never stay the same. The psalmist points out that the "mountains shake," "waters roar and foam," "kingdoms totter," and wars come and go. Our world is still like this. Presidents, dictators, and kingdoms still rise and fall. The earth still quakes, old familiar landmarks are torn down, children grow up and move on, rivers are dammed, ministers come and go, good friends die, and people move.

Isn't it extraordinary that the Bible was written by real people living in the real world? It was not written from some stained-glass fantasy. Nor was it written from some Eiffel Tower of idealism. It was written by common men in this tender, brutal world.

Because of this, it speaks eloquently to our needs if we but listen. Certainly one of our needs is a way of coping with change. If I had to list five main things that are destroying the earth today, I'd have to list rust, frost, wind, water, and pollution. But if I had to list five main things that are destroying peoples' lives, I'd have to list inability to adapt to change right up there with alcohol, money, pride, and selfishness. Change is devastating people! Because they can't cope with flux, their brittle lines are being snapped! A man loses his job, refuses to adjust, and quits at life. A couple's best friends get transferred, adjustments are called for, yet they are not willing to try. A mother's children grow up, leave home, and she is now empty.

There is always the human tendency to feel singled out, to feel that we alone live in a world of constant change, to feel that no one else has it hard like we do. The following is a bit of verse written by one such individual:

> *To whom can I speak today?*
> *The gentle man has perished,*
> *The violent man has access to everybody.*
> *To whom can I speak today?*
> *The iniquity that smites the land,*
> *It has no end.*
> *To whom can I speak today?*
> *There are no righteous men,*
> *The earth is surrendered to criminals.*

I suppose you're thinking that this lament must have been written by some New Yorker during the recent winter. No, it was written in Egypt 4,000 years ago by a man contemplating suicide. Singled out? Are we the only ones who've known a world of upheavals and change? No, this Egyptian felt it. The psalmist wrote about it and we know it, too. A French adage says, "The more things change, the more they remain the same." As it was in Egypt, so it is today.

The fact is that we live in a world of change. The question is, how do we react to these changes? A fellow got into a Washington, DC, taxi recently and said, "Driver, drive me back about twenty years!" Nostalgia is one way of dealing with flux. Complaining is another. "They don't make 'em like they used to!" "Back in my day...." "Ah, but those were the good old days, now, it's not so good!" "The world's going to the dogs!" Complain, complain, complain! One lady in her eighties, rigid and conservative about many things that the scriptures aren't even conservative about, had become cynical with modern life and the changes it brought. "Pastor," she whined, "it's a good time to be dead!"

Here's a little poem about the past. I think you'll agree that it rubs a little luster off the "good old days gone by."

> *Grandmother, on a winter's day*
> *Milked the cows and fed them hay*
> *Slopped the hogs, saddled the mule,*
> *And got the children off to school*
> *Did the washing, mopped the floors,*
> *Washed the windows and did some chores;*
> *Cooked a dish of home dried fruit,*
> *Pressed her husband's Sunday suit;*
> *Swept the parlor, made the beds,*
> *Baked a dozen loafs of bread;*
> *Split some firewood and lugged in*
> *Enough to fill the kitchen bin;*
> *Cleaned the lamps and put in oil,*
> *Stewed some apples she thought would spoil.*
> *Cooked a supper that was delicious,*
> *And afterwards washed up the dishes;*
> *Fed the cat and sprinkled the clothes,*
> *Mended a basket full of hose,*
> *Then opened the organ and began to play,*
> *"When you come to the end of a perfect day."*
> — Author unknown

I like that! It says it all! Contentment! Hard work in the present! Hearing about Grandma's winter day makes your back ache a bit, too, doesn't it? It makes one begin to think that maybe the good old days weren't so good after all! Who'd like to go back and relive the '60s with its Vietnam and riots? Or what about the '50s? Would you really like to return to the Jim Crow laws and Korea?

What about the '40s and Hitler or the '30s and the Depression? What about the Roaring '20s? Would you like to go back there and allow a dentist to work on your tooth? What about a decade before that? Let's see, that was World War I, wasn't it?

God Is In Control!

Yes, we live in a world of change. The psalmist points this out with his view of quaking mountains, surging tides, and tottering kingdoms. "The earth melts," he says. But our songwriter is quick to point out one clear and unchanging fact in this ever-changing world: God is in control. The psalmist says that the Lord can utter his voice and wars cease. He can break kingdoms, totter empires, and be in the midst of his people so that they shall not be moved. "I am exalted among the nations," God says. "I am exalted in the earth!" he exclaims.

Seeing such a God and believing his promises, the wordsmith of the psalms said, "God is our refuge and strength, a very present help in trouble. Therefore we will not fear though the earth should change." The psalmist had serenity about life and death and violence and change. We seem to have never found such contentment. My, my, how we can worry! How we can grumble and wax nostalgically, and what bitter cynics we can become!

Do you remember how it was when you were first married? You were afraid of your spouse's driving, weren't you? Every time you traveled, you made it a practice to take the wheel. They might take a wrong turn or run off the road or fail to note an instrument's warning. But then came that long journey, too long for you to drive it alone. They'd have to share the driving responsibilities with you. Remember how it was with them behind the wheel? Dog-tired as you were, you couldn't relax. You felt compelled to be a backseat driver. "Does she see that stop sign?" "Watch out for that cow!" "Slow down here!" Finally, fatigue outlasted you and you fell asleep to dream of fears and disasters, hardships and breakdowns. Then your wife woke you up with a shake to tell you that you had arrived safely at your destination. After a few trips like that, you began to believe in your wife's driving ability! Now you suspect that the old girl is a better driver than you! A lot of people go through life a backseat driver. They are full of anxiety because they don't trust God's ability. In the text, the psalmist was willing to leave the driving to God. He trusted the Lord's ability to remain in control of situations. He wasn't like so many of us, afraid to relax, afraid to sleep, for fear of what change might bring. He wasn't forever hitting the brakes, backseat driving, and fretting, "Slow down!" What about you? Can you sleep while your wife drives? Better still, can you relax with God at the wheel of the universe?

T. S. Eliot compared God to the North Star. Against a canopy of constellations in flux the North Star is a fixed point useful for navigation. Eliot wrote saying, "He is the still point of the turning world." The psalmist found that still point. He could confidently whisper, "God is our refuge and strength, a very present help in trouble. Therefore we will not fear though the earth should change." Perhaps the psalmist sensed our lack of adjustment, our tense response to the difference a day makes, for he turns to us in his psalm and speaks a word of God. "Be still. Be still and know that I am God." Aye! Here's a word for us! We've been so busy in our haste to live at top speed socially and economically that we've left our souls behind. That still point in a turning world, that pole star to chart our course by, is lost to our view. How do we find it? "Be still." Quit your selfish haste, your frantic worrying, that foolish rigidity! "Be still and know. Know that I am God. I make wars to cease. I burn the chariots of battle and totter kingdoms. With me as your refuge you shall not be moved!"

Martin Luther loved this psalm. He used it as the basis for his hymn, "A Mighty Fortress." In times of stress he'd say, "Let's go sing Psalm 46!" Along with Dr. Luther and the psalmist, we can say, "This! This is the day that the Lord hath made. Let us rejoice and be glad in it" (Psalm 118:24). With God at the wheel of the universe, we can relax. He's in control.

Make Change!

Yes, the world is changing, and yes, God is in control. We are also told that Christians should cause change. To his followers throughout history, Jesus Christ said, "Go and make disciples of all nations, baptizing them in the name of the Father, Son, and

Holy Spirit, teaching them to observe all that I have commanded you." This verse is known as the Great Commission. You are aware of how a king will commission an artist to do a sculpture. He will give him a block of marble and say, "Create for me a statue of David," and Michelangelo will go to work changing that stone into artistic splendor. With God and us it is the same. The Lord commissions us, his artists, to preach the gospel, to baptize in the Holy Spirit, and to teach all nations to observe God's law. He commissions us to win people to Christ. These then changed people will change the world!

During my college days in the 1960s, I studied in England. While in London, I applied for a visa to visit the Soviet Union. I wanted to leave in two weeks. The agent at the Russian Embassy told me that it was impossible to gain a visa in two weeks. Still, I insisted that I try. He gave me the papers and I filled them out. One question said, "Occupation?" I didn't want to put Christian minister because that would be frowned on, I thought, by Russian officials. So, brash as I was, I simply wrote down "Revolutionary." I got the visa a week later. Looking back now on that question, "What is your occupation?" I feel that my answer may have been more correct than I first thought. I am a revolutionary! All Christians are. I'm committed to death to preach the gospel. I am committed with fervent zeal to bringing people into a life changing relationship with Jesus Christ. I am committed to changing families, morals, politics, and society the world over — starting with myself.

The Bible teaches that God created the universe in six days. On day seven he rested. But then creation rebelled against the Lord and fell to pieces like a shattered mirror. But now Jesus says, "My Father is working still" (John 5:17). Day seven is over! God no longer rests. This is the eighth day of creation. Christ is at work restoring humanity's broken relationship with God, self, neighbor, and creation. Our Father is working still. He's not satisfied with the world as it is, and he invites us, through the Great Commission, to work with him to change the world.

Let's face it. The church has fallen short here. The church too often fights change rather than makes change. The church can become a protector of the status quo, a defender of only the kings on the mountains. But God's will is not just to keep things the way they are right now. Sure, the world has been good to us. We're Americans. We've got food and jobs and health and power. We even know something of Jesus. But we are a minority here on earth. For the majority of humanity, there is little food, poor health, inadequate shelter, and no chance to hear the gospel. Hence, God commissions us to work with him as change agents.

Look at it this way. There can be no life without growth. Progress, maturity, improvements, development — all these things are impossible without change. This world today, even at its best, is still substandard. God is not satisfied with it the way it is. He calls us out of our stained glass fox holes, our bastions of nostalgia, our snugness as a bug-in-a-rug in the status quo, and he says, "Christian, make change! Work with me to make this world better until Christ returns to make it the best it can be!"

A notable Ivy League college president once said, "I divide the people of the world into three categories. There is a group of people that watch things happen. There is the overwhelming majority that doesn't even know what is happening. There is that small committed minority that makes things happen." We Christians have not been called to the status quo, nor have we been called to ignorance or apathy. We belong to that small committed minority that makes change for the better happen.

You Can't Beat It! Join It!

In a *Peanuts* cartoon, Snoopy is moping atop his doghouse. "I feel it," he says. "I feel it. Change is in the air." Then a golden leaf falls from a tree and Snoopy is quick up to catch it. Another leaf falls and then another and another and another. Snoopy is frantic. He tries to blow the leaves back up in the air. After a futile hour's work Snoopy sighs and returns to his doghouse. "Oh, well," he says. "Winter will come. Change is inevitable." What about you? Are you like Snoopy? Are you wishing for a world that does not exist, that never changes? God has not given us such a home! Change is a fact of life. You can't beat it, but you can join it! With Christ, we can return again to the cutting edge of society. With the psalmist, we can talk about the good now days! "This! This is the day that the Lord hath made. Let us rejoice and be glad in it," as we make change!

Suggested Prayer
Father God, let me remember that to be loud is not to be right; to be strange is not to be forbidden; to be new is not to be frightful. Lord, grant me the courage to change the things that need changing, the serenity to accept the things that do not need changing, and the wisdom to know the difference. For Christ's sake. Amen.

Psalm 107

No More Stingy Hosannas

O give thanks to the Lord for he is good; for his steadfast love endures for ever!
— Psalm 107:1

"My thanksgiving is stingy this year," he confided. "My life is like a flashlight with weak batteries. It makes a feeble light." And don't we know how he feels, ourselves spent with living? What we need is a recharge from God's word. More specifically, we need a recharge from Psalm 107.

This particular psalm is an ancient Hebrew poem. Its author was one who knew life with all its joys and sorrows, disappointments and heartaches. He'd tasted the sweetness of life, but also its bitter dregs. He set himself down to paper with pen to express it all.

Psalm 107 is a tightly written hymn that easily falls into three parts. First, there is the prologue in verses 1-3, a call to thanksgiving. Second, there are four stanzas of the hymn, each giving a glimpse of life, verses 4-31. Note carefully the formula each hymn stanza follows. A difficult portion of life is described — "Some wandered in desert ways." God's transforming grace is exclaimed — "He led them in a straight way." And then there is the resulting praise — "Let them thank the Lord for his steadfast love." That, the prologue, four stanzas, and now this. Third, the epilogue in verses 32-43, a quiet testimony to God's providence.

With this background, let's go into the psalm itself.

Man, The Pilgrim

The first stanza paints a word picture of man, the pilgrim. "Some wandered in desert wastes, finding no way to a city to dwell in; hungry and thirsty, their soul fainted within them."

This description of life is a page right out of Jewish history! Abraham wandered the fertile crescent from Babylon to Egypt. Living in tents, he faced heat, floods, famine, and war. You might say he was a forerunner of the modern business executive. (Someone told me, "IBM stands for I've Been Moved.")

Today, people are on the move as never before. Refugees, immigrants, vacationers — I myself have traveled over 110,000 miles in one year on everything from a car to a boat to a jet. Along the old Oregon Trail out west is a huge stone mountain called "Message Rock." Settlers passing through would often carve their names there to let others coming behind them know of their progress. "Honus Bishop passed through here 6/52," one reads. There you have it! Man, the pilgrim, passing through life.

But where is man going? Why is he traveling? On a jet in Texas, two women boarded, took their seats, and spoke to the pilot as he passed. "Don't fly faster than the speed of sound," one said. "We want to talk!" So many of us are like that today. We live in the fast lane and never stop to ask directions. And like the psalmist says, we "wander," "in the desert," "hungry and thirsty," with "no city to dwell in." Clearly, the psalmist is saying that man, the pilgrim, is lost!

The confusion of life, the fatigue of the rat race, the hurt of taking that downhill byway that seemed so attractive, but ended up in drugs or the occult or loneliness — these are all too familiar to many of us. Matthew Arnold wrote, "Most men eddy about here and there; eat and drink, chatter and love and hate, gather and squander, are raised aloft and hurled in the dust, strive blindly, achieving nothing and then they die — perish. And no one asks who or what they have been more than he asks what waves in the moonlight solitudes mild of the midmost ocean have swelled, foamed for a moment and gone."

We are such pilgrims — lost, weary, fainting. As Israel wandered forty years in the wilderness, we today can wander the wastelands for seventy years or more. Such is life, the poet says.

But then there is a transforming stroke of the pen! "Then they cried to the Lord in their trouble and he delivered them from their distress; he led them by a straight way, till they reached a city to dwell in" (vv. 6-7). Man is the pilgrim, yes! But that is not the entire story. For man is a pilgrim God can guide!

What of yourself? Have you met the shepherd of life, Jesus, the Christ? My wife and I, touring Ireland by car years ago, were lost on back roads. We stopped to ask a stranger, "Do you know the way to Tralee?" He smiled and said, "You're not lost. You've found me! And I know the way!" It is the same when one meets Jesus. "I know the way," he proclaims of himself. Man, the pilgrim, becomes one whom God guides along a straight path.

Now the poem bursts into the resulting praise, "Let them thank the Lord for his steadfast love, for his wonderful works to the sons of men! For he satisfies him who is thirsty, and hungry he fills with good things."

Man, The Prisoner

The second stanza gives us the picture of man, the prisoner. "Some sat in darkness and in gloom, prisoners in affliction and in irons, for they had rebelled against the words of God, and spurned the counsel of the most high God. Their hearts were bowed down with hard labor. They fell down with none to help" (vv. 10-12).

Again, this is Israel's history — slaves making bricks for Pharaoh in Egypt. They were enslaved by Assyria, by Babylon, by Rome, and by Nazi Germany. Life is like this, the poet is saying. Man is still the prisoner today — imprisoned in materialism that gives our spirit no room to breathe. We are imprisoned by conformity, drugs, and secular triviality. Some know their plight and desperately try to claw their way out. Others never realize their confinement at all, living the one-dimensional existence of a roach in a dungeon.

Man is a prisoner — if not by drugs, then by habits or things or the past or demons. Rousseau wrote, "Man was born free, but everywhere he is in chains!" "Prisoners in irons," the psalmist says. "Hearts bowed down with hard labor." "They fall with none to lift them up."

But now comes a transforming stroke of the poet's pen! "Then they cried to the Lord in their trouble, and he delivered them out of their distress. He brought them out of darkness and gloom, and broke their bonds asunder" (vv. 13-14). Man is the prisoner, yes. But man is also a prisoner God can set free!

Fundamentally, the gospel of Jesus Christ is a message of release. In Luke 4:18, Jesus goes into the synagogue to preach his first sermon: "The Spirit of the Lord is upon me," he proclaims, "because he has anointed me to preach good news to the poor, he has sent me to proclaim release to the captives, and recovering of sight to the blind, to set at liberty those who are oppressed...."

Visitors in our church most frequently comment on how free a people we are! And I tell them, "If the Son of Man shall make you free, you shall be free indeed!" Free from bad habits; free to live good habits; free to laugh, to cry, to be weak; free to ask questions and grow — all these are Christ's doings, and it is beautiful in our sight. "He brought them out of darkness and gloom, and broke their bonds asunder."

Again comes the thrill of resulting praise. "Let them thank the Lord for his steadfast love, for his wonderful words to the sons of men! For he shatters the doors of bronze, and cuts in two the bars of iron."

Man, The Sufferer

A third portrait comes in stanza three — man, the sufferer. "Some were sick through their sinful ways, and because of their iniquities suffered affliction; they loathed any kind of food and they drew near to the gates of death" (vv. 17-18).

Again we hear the history of the Jews echoed: their plagues, their pestilence, fever, and death. "You are dust and to dust you shall return."

Novelist Stephen Crane wrote, "A man said to the universe, 'Sir, I exist.' 'However,' replied the universe, 'the fact has not created in me a sense of obligation.' " Goya, the nineteenth-century artist, has a painting titled, *The executions of 3rd May, 1808*. There is a firing squad of machinelike Napoleonic troops, their backs to us. Unarmed peasants are herded against a wall, their faces terrified, in despair, one praying. The bodies of friends are fallen in bloody heaps. The sky is closed in darkness. A lifeless church spire rises in the distant background. The soldiers methodically do their killing. No one is available to rescue the peasants and one poor man stands in the middle and raises his arms as if in the position of one being crucified.

Man, the sufferer. We are such poor ailing creatures eaten by sin's cancer. We try to effect a cure, yet sin stubbornly refuses to yield! Communist defector and novelist, Arthur Koestler, wrote *Darkness at Noon*. In it, an aging Communist party boss, fallen from power, is arrested, imprisoned, and tortured psychologically. He sits in his solitary cell wondering where things went wrong.

> *The cause of the party's defectiveness must be found. All our principles were right, but our results were wrong. This is a diseased century. We diagnosed the disease and its causes with microscopic exactness, but wherever we applied the healing knife, a new sore appeared. Our will was hard and pure, we should have even been loved by the people. But they hate us. Why are we so odious and detested? We brought you truth, but in our mouths it sounded like a lie. We brought you freedom, and it looks in our hands like a whip. We brought you the living life, and where our voice is heard, the trees wither and there is a rustling of dry leaves....*[1]

Again, man is the sufferer — born in pain, dying in pain, and living the in-between in pain. But again this is not the end of the story! For with a stroke of his pen, man, the sufferer, becomes man, the sufferer, whom God can heal. "Then they cried to the Lord in their trouble, and he delivered them from their distress. He sent forth his word and healed them and delivered them from destruction."

God has not been in our sufferings, healing barrenness, loneliness, ignorance, bodily injury, spiritual darkness, depression, insecurity, low self-esteem, and more? So, now, the reverberating praise, "Let them thank the Lord for his steadfast love, for his wonderful works to the sons of men ... And let them offer sacrifices of thanksgiving, and tell of his deeds in songs of joy!" (vv. 8, 22).

Man, The Voyager

So far we've read of man, the pilgrim, whom God can lead; man, the prisoner, whom God can free; and man, the sufferer whom God can heal. Now, in the fourth stanza, we meet man, the voyager.

> *Some went down to the sea in ships, doing business on the great waters; they saw the deeds of the Lord, his wondrous works in the deep. For he commanded, and raised the stormy wind, which lifted up the waves of the sea. They mounted up to heaven, they went down to the depth; their courage melted away in their evil plight; they reeled and staggered like drunken men, and were at their wits' end.* — Psalm 107:23-27

Obviously, one can see that Jewish people feared the ocean. It was understood as a place of evil, of treachery and uncertainty. For these reasons, Jews did not travel the oceans very much.

When the poet mentions doing business on a turbulent sea, we can immediately identify with the ups and downs of business. Certainly, the stock market has experienced storm waves. In all of life, our fortunes rise and sink until we ourselves are staggered, drowned, and dead.

Thus man is a voyager on a troubled sea toward death. But what follows death? Is there no safe harbor to anchor in?

In a New England cemetery, an epitaph reads, "Stranger! Approach this spot with gravity! Joe Brown, Dentist, is filling his last cavity." And another, "Under this stone, reader, survey dead architect, John Vanbrough's house of clay. Lie heavy on him, earth! For he laid many heavy loads on thee."

French impressionist, Paul Gaugain's last painting before his suicide attempt had these words painted in a darker corner of his work, "Whence? What? Whither? Fate, how cruel thou art!"

The same question is found in Russia during World War II, in which twenty million of her sons and daughters were slain. An anonymous poem, "Do Not Call Me" has survived.

Do not call me, Father. Do not seek me.
Do not call me. Do not wish me back.
We're on a route uncharted.
Fire and blood erase our track.
On we fly on wings of thunder never more to sheath
our swords.
All of us in battle fallen, not to be brought back by words.
Will there be a rendezvous? I know not.
I only know we still must fight.
We are sand grains in infinity, never to meet,
Never more see life.

Man is the voyager toward death. But this is not the entire story. For with a stroke of his pen, the sweet psalmist of Israel writes, "Then they cried to the Lord in their trouble and he delivered them from their distress ... He made the storm be still, and the waves of the sea were hushed ... He brought them to their desired haven" (vv. 19, 29, 30b). Thus man, the voyager, becomes man, the voyager whom God can bring through death to a safe haven. Christ has done this for us by his life, death, and resurrection. "Neither let them be afraid. Let not your hearts be troubled. I go to prepare a place for you" (John 14:2, 27).

What must it be like to step on shore and find heaven? To take hold of a steadying hand, and find it Christ's? To breathe new air, and find it celestial? To feel invigorated, and find it immortality? To rise from the care, the loneliness, and turmoil of earth into one unbroken calm, to wake up and find it glory and heaven?

I tell you, there is but one fitting response! "Let them thank the Lord for his steadfast love, for his wonderful works to the sons of men! Let them extol him in the congregation of people and praise him in the assembly of the elders."

Conclusion

So, we have four images of man — the pilgrim, the prisoner, the sufferer, and the voyager. Such is life, the psalmist writes. But for every pain of life, Christ offers a corresponding grace. The pilgrim can be led, the prisoner set free, the sufferer healed, and the voyager brought to a safe harbor. All of this God is doing for you and for me in Christ Jesus our Lord!

But what of our response? I'm convinced that our thanksgiving to God for his grace is far too stingy. That is why the psalmist penned this hymn. Eight times he urges us to gratitude, "O that men would thank the Lord for his steadfast love, for his wonderful works to the sons of men."

This psalm can be the cure for our appallingly feeble and stingy hosannas year round. It ends with the directive, "Whoever is wise, let him give heed to these things; let men consider the steadfast love of the Lord."

At a Bill Glass Christian Crusade in Kentucky in 1970, a political activist visited. "How do you get your people so excited?" the political worker asked the preacher.

"If you could get your candidate to do for people what Jesus has done for men, you wouldn't have any trouble either!" he said.

"O that men would thank the Lord for his steadfast love, for his wonderful works to the sons of men."

Suggested Prayer

Lord, take my wanderings, my pain, my shackles, and my voyage. Make me yours in Christ that I might ever praise your name. Amen.

---

1. Arthur Koestler, *Darkness at Noon* (New York: Scribner, 2006), p. 59.

Psalm 120

Forward, Retreat!

> *In my distress, I cry to the Lord, that he may answer me: "Deliver me, O Lord, from lying lips, from a deceitful tongue."*
> *What shall be given to you? And what more done to you, you deceitful tongue? A warrior's sharp arrows, with glowing coals of the broom tree!*
> *Woe is me, that I sojourn in Meshech, that I dwell among the tents of Kedar! Too long have I had my dwelling among those who hate peace. I am for peace; but when I speak, they are for war!*   — Psalm 120

"Forward, retreat!" That may sound like a strange order, but sometimes the way forward is backward. Example: You're chopping wood for the winter. You have been at it nearly a month and by now your ax is dull. You need to stop and sharpen it, but you don't want to quit chopping wood. Yet, until you turn aside and sharpen your tool, you can't really go forward with your purpose.

In my line of work, we have a saying: "An amateur is a person so busy chopping wood he never stops to sharpen his own ax." So, dull and tired, he flails away. He is involved for sure, but largely ineffective.

And so it is with the man who wrote Psalm 120, the first of the vacationers' psalms. Today we would call the man "a victim of burnout." In seven short verses he uses words like "distress," "cry," "lying lips," "deceitful tongue," "warrior's sharp arrows," "woe," "hate peace," "war," and "too long." The key to all this woe is "too long." "Too long have I had my dwelling among those who hate peace." Too long has he been involved. Too long has he labored without letting up. Too long has he gone without a holiday.

If you scrutinize this psalm carefully, you'll see that this man has got his eyes more on people than he does on God. In the Bible, we are essentially told to stare at God and glance at people. But this man is staring at people and glancing at God. And the results are fatigue, negativism, and making mountains out of molehills and molehills out of mountains.

In literary form, Psalm 120 is what is known as a lament. It is a human expression of grief, of frustration and despair.

In Distress

Notice that this psalm begins with the words, "In my distress." Most scholars ascribe this psalm to David, saying that it was probably written when Doeg falsely accused him to Saul. That painful episode is described in 1 Samuel 21 and 22.

Saul is the king. But he is unrighteous and God has promised to tear the kingdom from him. The prophet Samuel has gone ahead and anointed David king instead. Though David is not crowned yet, God's hand is clearly evident in his life. He has already slain the giant, Goliath; written poetry; routed the Philistines; and mastered the musical instrument known as the lyre.

Saul has become jealous and seeks to kill David. So David flees into the wilderness — hounded, hungry, thirsty, and tired.

That's when he comes to the village of Nob. There the priests feed and rest him and give him Goliath's old sword and send him on his way.

Yet, in the corner is a man watching. He is Saul's chief herdsman, a man who sees in David an opportunity to promote himself before Saul. His name is Doeg, and he "rats" on David. He tells King Saul of the priests' helpfulness and of David's whereabouts.

Saul is appreciative of Doeg's helpfulness and outraged at the priests of Nob. He orders his soldiers to kill them. But they refuse. "I can't kill a priest, an unarmed man, a holy one!" So Doeg, ever alert to be a man pleaser, takes a sword and says, "I'll do it!" He slays 85 men of God. Then he leads in the destruction of the village of Nob and sees that even the women and children are slain.

But as the story goes, one of the priests escapes to David's camp and brings the terrible news. David's heart is broken. "I have occasioned the death of all the people of your father's house," he grieves. Somewhere in the night, this fugitive boy king pens Psalm 120, a lament and a prayer for deliverance.

Can we not identify with David's distress? For each of us there is a heaping portion of distress. We, too, have been put on trial behind our backs. We, too, have had to live, at one time or another, in an atmosphere fraught with tension, suspicion, intrigue, and deceit. Do you know what it is like to be an anointed king and not be crowned yet? To live with unfulfilled longings? To live between what is and what is to be? Do you know what it is to live life on the run, to be followed with malice, hounded, and have to fight your way through life?

This was David's life. Separated from his best friend, Jonathan, on the run, living in an inhospitable place — the desert, having to fight for his very existence. And when finally someone is nice to him, when a priest offers him lodging, food, and drink, and a sword, it all ends in misery and slaughter with David feeling responsible. "If only I had not gone there...." If you've never been a leader, if you've never had to make hard decisions that hurt others, then you'll never quite know the pain David surely felt in all of this.

"Woe is me," David wrote, "that I sojourn in Meshech, that I dwell among the tents of Kedar." Kedar is in the desert regions of Damascus, while Meshech is in present-day Turkey. Both were pagan lands far from Israel, places where David had never been. What David is saying is, "I don't live in Israel, in God's kingdom. Far from it. I live in a distant pagan wasteland!" It would be like one of us becoming disgusted with our church and people's behavior, and griping, "Woe is me! I live in the Bronx or Beirut! Life around here is about that far from the way God does things!"

I Cried

So David begins with "in my distress," and then he adds, "I cried" — "In my distress I cried."

Certainly, in reading all of David's psalms one must conclude he was an expressive man of God, honest with his feelings. Unlike so many, David did not pretend. He did not hide or suppress his feelings. He was vulnerable.

Jesus was like that, too. The shortest verse in the Bible says, "Jesus wept." When Lazarus, his friend, died, Jesus cried.

The simple truth of the matter is that Jews, God's chosen people, are very demonstrative with their feelings. If they are happy, they smile, laugh, clap their hands, and even dance. If they are sad, they cry, they wail, tear their garments, and heap ashes on their heads. In short, they feel their feelings and express themselves honestly.

Contrast that with us today. We hold it all inside, saying, "I'm tough. I must not let my feelings show!" We call it "being reserved." The Bible calls it being dishonest with yourself, with God, and with others. Doctors call it sick.

You see, if one does not cry outwardly, he will cry inwardly. If honest communication does not flow, if feelings are not adequately expressed, then emotions build up inside like the pressures in a mighty volcano. And there will come a day when it all explodes.

How well I recall my daughter falling and scraping her knee when she was but a five-year-old. And my, oh my, but how she cried. So I took her in my arms and tried to comfort her, saying, "Don't cry, honey. It'll be okay." And she looked at me and said, "But, Daddy, I have to cry. It lets the hurt out." And so it does.

Psalm 120 is saying that just maybe good vacations begin with a good cry.

I Cry To The Lord

"In my distress," David said, "I cry." But more specifically, "I cry to the Lord." Here is a man who knows where to go for help! He knows the secret of prayer.

I have a neighbor who has lived in Burlington, North Carolina, all his life. And I've learned that he really knows his way around. He knows the best plumber, the best tree service, electricians, roofers, and repairmen. So when I need a fixer and don't know where to call for help, I ask my neighbor for a tip.

Psalm 120 shows us that David knew his way around the universe. He lived there! And when he needed help, he knew where to go! "In my distress I cried to the Lord." He prayed about it. He poured out his soul to God.

Elizabeth Elliot tells of a brother who was a missionary to the Indians of Alaska. Six or seven of the men in his area had banded together for mutual support. There came a time when the group was wanting to elect him president of their group. During the month for elections, a fellow missionary sent a letter to the others slandering him and pointing out how unfit he was. Actually, the accuser just wanted the job for himself.

Well, what to do? Should he send out his own letter? Should he lower himself to the standard of his slanderer and slander him back? The missionary simply went into his prayer room, spread the letter out before God, and poured out all his hurts and frustration. And there with God, he left things, got up, and went on about his work.

As God chose to work it out, the slanderous man was not elected, Elizabeth's brother was. Within the year, the accuser had quit and left the mission field.

He Answers

"In my distress, I cry to the Lord," David confessed. He didn't cry to King Saul or to Doeg or his wife. He cried to God. David tells us why: "In my distress I cry to the Lord, that he may answer me."

Here is a real question for you and for me today. When we are hurt with life, whom do we really want to answer our needs? Do we want a banker — Dear Abby — a pastor — a wife or friend — or Jesus? What it really comes down to is how well you really know your way around the universe and whom you've come to believe is both able and available to meet your needs.

Once, a family had a big party, and the children were allowed to watch television while Mom and Dad mingled with their guests around the pool. About 9:30 p.m., little six-year-old Timmy, sure that he wasn't getting enough attention, walked poolside and announced for all to hear, "I'm going upstairs to say my bedtime prayers. Does anybody want anything?" He was onto something! Philippians 2:5-7 teaches that though Jesus was God, he humbled himself and took on the form of a servant. More particularly, he humbled himself to serve you — even to wash your feet or to die on the cross for your sins. A real secret of prayer is in realizing that Jesus Christ is a servant who is ready, willing, and able to serve you that you might serve him.

Enemies Punished

Next, David goes on to say that his enemies will be punished. Thus, Psalm 120, among other things, is a reminder that we live in a just universe. Retribution will come. It may seem slow, but it is sure.

King Saul, that unrighteous monarch who so hounded David and quenched the Spirit of God, was to perish in battle atop Mount Gilboa, a victim of his own sword thrust. And Doeg? What of this conniving man pleaser? He is not mentioned after the massacre at Nob. He simply fades into anonymity, perhaps to die in battle with the Saul whose coattails he sought to ride from herdsman to the king's court. For both of them it was as the Greeks observed centuries ago: "Though the mills of the gods grind slowly, they grind exceedingly fine."

David talks about God's revenge in verses 3 and 4. "What shall be given to you? And what more shall be done to you, you deceitful tongue?" he asks. And then the answer: "A warrior's sharp arrows, with glowing coals of the broom tree!" In other words, those who've shed innocent blood at Nob will die by "a warrior's sharp arrows" and their bodies will be buried with "glowing coals of the broom tree." Some quick insight is needed here: The broom tree is a thorny juniper tree. When its wood is ignited, it does not flame up fast. Instead, it burns very hot, yet slowly and thoroughly. Even after a few days, the ashes still hold their heat. So, what David is saying is that men like Doeg and Saul are turned over to God's wrath that consumes them like a long, hot, thorough fire.

I will share with you something personal. I'd really rather not share it at all, but Spirit says to do so. I share it with humility, with fear, and with trembling.

Many years ago, a few men like Doeg destroyed a church ministry I was involved in. And, as at Nob, many innocent people were wounded and slain. Looking back, I now see the vengeance almighty God has taken on his detractors. The ringleader went into the hospital, got pneumonia, and died. Another had an affair, his wife divorced him, and to settle, he had to sell his business that put his two sons out on the street. Another was struck dead by a car while crossing the street. Yet another has continued deeper into alcoholism and was given an early retirement from his church. One more was dismissed from his pulpit and has disappeared into obscurity.

Isn't that awesome? Does it not put a healthy fear into each of our lives that we might live faithfully and flee God's wrath ourselves?

Peace

So here is David's lament, the hymn of a man who needs a rest. "In my distress I cry to the Lord, that he may answer me" and deal with my enemies in his slow, hot, thorough burning wrath. But in this psalm, it is not enough to ask what happened to Doeg and Saul, what is the destiny of sinners. We must also ask what is to be done with David; what is the destiny of the righteous?

Verse 7 gives a clue. There David says, "I am for peace." As ever, the Hebrew word for "peace" is *shalom*. It means more than the absence of war. It means also the presence of righteousness, justice, good crops, economic health, and the like.

Today, we speak of peace in terms of *utopia*, which is a Greek word meaning "nowhere." Literally, nowhere on this earth is peace and prosperity! Yet, we still search for it! Man tried to build peace or *utopia* with reason alone in the Brooks Farm Experiment. Marx tried to build it with communism: "From each according to his ability, to each according to his need." We've even tried to do it here in the United States with a constitutional republic, a "government of the people, by the people, for the people." And both history and scripture are clear: Peace is not something man made. It is God made. It is not something that is here now. It is something coming in the future. Or as Revelation 21:2 says, it is a fellowship, a *koinonia*, a city built by God let down out of heaven to earth. And this is to be our destiny with David in Christ. Ultimately, we shall live in peace. No more Saul or Doeg or deserts or swords or unfulfilled longings.

Conclusion

In conclusion, look carefully at how this psalm ends. David is a man involved. He is living his faith in community. But he is tired, hounded, frustrated, and even negative. Nevertheless, he looks to God and is heard. His heart is filled with longing for peace and he is about to begin a journey toward it.

Verse 5 has the key word of the psalm for our need in today's world. It is "sojourner." It means "a traveler, a homeless one on his way, or someone passing through." "I sojourn," David said. "I'm homeless, passing through, a traveler with God toward peace."

That should be our attitude toward this life we live as well. An old gospel song says, "The world is not my home." A nineteenth-century maxim says, "Life is a bridge. Cross over it. Enjoy the walk and the view. But don't try to build your home on it." Yet today we tend to try to make ourselves comfortable with life, to quit sojourning and settle down.

Robert Louis Stevenson once wrote, "The world is so full of a number of things, I'm sure we should all be as happy as kings!" We can be if we're not careful.

Many years ago, my wife and I, newlyweds, spent the night on a big brass bed in a Scottish castle. Before we went to sleep, my wife turned to me in the dark and said, "Stephen, it'd sure be hard to die if we had all of this!" The world and all that is in the world can constitute a very strong, almost irresistible pull on God's people. The tension between what is now and what will be is at times almost unendurable. It is tempting to trade future hope for present satisfaction, to settle for half best now rather than the best later, to settle into the temporal and forget the eternal. Many Christians today are doing this. Rather than yearning for God's peace, they settle for what is materially the best, here and now, rather than live and wait for the city of God.

David reminds us from his own life: Things aren't right. This is not the place. We must be a pilgrim, on the move, going up!

Suggested Prayer

Lord, take my hand and walk with me through all the stresses of life. For Jesus' sake. Amen.

Psalm 126

How To Heal With Humor

> *When the Lord restored the fortunes of Zion, we were like those who dream. Then our mouth was filled with laughter, and our tongue with shouts of joy....*
> — Psalm 126:1-2

A man went to see a psychiatrist. He was lonely, depressed, and joyless. The doctor listened for half an hour, then prescribed, "What you need is a good laugh. And I know just the thing! Last night I went to the circus. And there is a clown there who is hilarious. I suggest you go to see him."

"But I cannot!" the patient protested.

"And, why not?" the psychiatrist asked.

"Because I am that clown."

In the beginning of the twenty-first century, behind our makeup, our superbly manicured lawns, and exciting social schedules, we are still a people who pretend. Though we've lost our laughter, we still put on a pretty good show. Yet, deep down, we wonder, "What's so funny?"

Modern man is desperate for a laugh! Editors place cartoons in the pages of our magazines. Each newspaper has its funny pages. Television has its situation comedies with their laugh tracks, and here in the city, you may even rent a clown to enliven your party.

Yet, it's all a losing effort! One quarter of the American population will suffer some form of serious depression during the next two years. Nuclear weapons will continue to proliferate, child abuse will increase, the economy will slump deeper into debt, and many will handle the gloom by committing suicide, making it the number two killer of young people ages fifteen to 35.

The fact is, humor is ill and doesn't get around much anymore. When's the last time you had a good belly laugh? Is joy a heaping portion of your day today?

It is as if our nation, desperate as she is for a good time, has been robbed of her sense of humor. It's as if we are under a judgment! Jeremiah 16:9 explains it all, "For thus says the Lord of hosts, the God of Israel: Behold, I will make to cease from this place, before your eyes and in your days, the voice of mirth and the voice of gladness...." From where I sit, it looks as though this very thing has happened to us!

The good news is that God is more eager to give laughter than he is sorrow. The text even says God can fill our mouths with laughter and our tongues with shouts of joy!

The Hebrew word most often used for laughter is *tsachaq*, which means "to have merriment, to make sport, or to play." The Greek word is *gelao* and it means "a sign of joy, satisfaction, or a mark of gratification." Modern Christians need desperately to get a balance on these things in our lives. For such a balance, let's turn to the Bible and see what it has to say about laughter.

Those Who Laugh At Nothing

First of all, there are those who laugh at nothing. Like Jeremiah 16:9 prophesies, God has removed from them the voice of mirth. Their answer to the question, "What's so funny?" is "Nothing! Absolutely nothing!"

You might remember when cars rode on hard rubber tires with no shocks. Every bump in the road produced a teeth-jarring thud until bald tires were replaced with air-cushioned tires that rode on shock absorbers. People without a sense of humor experience life without the cushion that humor provides. Henry Ward Beecher said it so well, "A man without mirth is like a wagon without springs, in which one is caused a disagreeable jolt by every pebble over which he passes."

Such people talk about taking everything so seriously as if it all depended on them. Nuclear war, famine, teen suicide, child abuse, herpes, AIDS, the deficit, and death.

You might recall the man of Greek mythology named Atlas who was doomed by the gods to hold the weight of the world upon his shoulders. This is what many of us do today. We take it all upon ourselves! It is philosophical humanism that preaches God is dead, or at best, unavailable, so man will have to do it all himself. So many, buying into this worldview, step forward to take full responsibility for the entire world and immediately lose their sense of humor. We're like Shakespeare's character who stands up and says, "I am Sir Oracle, and when I ope' my lips, let no dog bark!"[1]

It's been interesting to debate with feminists the abortion issue on campus. The thing I've noticed most about these women is their intensity. They think their cause and their rights are the most important things in the world. Seriousness crowds out all banter. And though they'll never laugh with you, they'll resent you every time.

Beware of those who laugh at nothing!

Those Who Laugh At Everything

The other extreme of humor in out day is those who laugh at everything.

For some, life is simply one big joke. Thus, everything is reduced to the convivial atmosphere of a fraternity party. John Belushi popularized this lifestyle in the movie, *Animal House*. Education, sex, authority, the law, eating — it was all treated with lurid, bawdy humor, and many follow his example.

On a more classic note, Ludwig Von Beethoven did the same thing in his famous *Ninth Symphony*. Beethoven took a really inferior poem by the German poet, Schiller, and set it to superior music. In the symphonic finale, called the "hymn of joy," Beethoven looses the voices of a choir and dozens of varied instruments to celebrated man-centered joy. For some few minutes, everybody sucks and blows, plucks, sings, and reaches for every rousing sound of joy they can find until the tune is done and they slump exhausted in their seats. Beethoven's life was like that. Rejecting God, he determined to go it alone, making personal gratification his one aim in life. And it all ended on his deathbed with his final words, "The comedy is ended!"

Christ even experienced this in his day as he went to heal a little girl who was sick unto death. Arriving at the house, the crowd told him not to bother because the child was already dead. When Jesus said he'd heal her anyway, "they laughed at him" (Luke 8:53). There you have it: We are people who don't believe God is relevant or capable. We are people who are willing to laugh at Jesus, at death, at life — at everything. Ours is a world full of such humor, today! Sarcasm, cynicism, gallows humor, whistling in the dark, dirty jokes, endless banter — for some it never ends. It would do us all good to read and take to life the following scriptures.

> *If a wise man has an argument with a fool, the fool only rages and laughs, and there is no quiet.*
> — Proverbs 26:18-19

> *Like a madman who throws firebrands, arrows, and death, is the man who deceives his neighbor and says, "I am only joking!"* — Proverbs 29:9

James counsels such people ...

> *Let your laughter be turned to mourning and your joy to dejection.* — James 4:9

On one hand, it seems there are those who laugh at nothing, while on the other hand, there are those who laugh at everything. And where is the balance? Where is the proportion Solomon talked about in Ecclesiastes?

> *For everything there is a season, and a time for every matter under heaven ... A time to weep and a time to laugh ... and he has made everything beautiful in its time.* — Ecclesiastes 3:1-4, 11

Laughing With God

Perhaps you've never thought of God as the ultimate source of humor, but it's time you do. For the Bible, in numerous places, not only says that God laughs, but it also enjoins us to laugh with him in the things with which he takes delight.

God laughs at man's rebellion. Psalm 2 describes man's rebellion against God. "The kings of the earth set themselves against the Lord, let us break his chains on us!" How does God respond? "He who sits in the heavens laughs; the Lord has them in derision."

Every year about this time, I have a good laugh as I encounter a sophomore student on campus who has had religion 101, sociology 103, biology 107, and history 110. He's doing a twelve-page term paper that is due next week and he tells me that if I will give him but thirty minutes, he and his term paper can explain away God, Jesus, the church, scripture, and guilt. "What do you think of that?" he asks assuredly. I usually shrug and say, "Oh, I think about the same thing of you as I would a flea sitting atop Mount Everest who shouts, 'Hey! Watch me! I'm going to kick down this entire mountain in twenty minutes with my left hind leg.' "

Our strength as humans is that we can laugh at ourselves for being so ridiculous. Our weakness is that we need to do it so often.

God laughs at our redemption. Luke 15 tells a story in which God identifies with the father of a runaway child who decides to come home. The dad immediately throws a party in which there is feasting and dancing and laughter. And Jesus said, "Just so, I tell you, there will be more joy in heaven over one sinner who repents ..." (Luke 15:7).

God laughs at our rebellion. He also laughs when we are redeemed.

God laughs at the routine of life. Genesis 17:17—21:6 tells the story of Abraham and Sarah and the birth of their first son. Advanced in years, yet childless, they long for a baby. And just when it seems too late, God said, "About this time next year I will visit you and you shall have a child." Whereupon Abraham literally falls on his face laughing (17:17). When he tells Sarah, she giggles and says, "Shall an old lady have pleasure?" And when the child comes, she names him Isaac, which is a Hebrew word meaning "laughter."

It is interesting in all of this that Abraham's wife loses her name Sarai to gain the name Sarah. Sarai means "contentious." But Sarah means "princess." And thus did laughter turn a beautiful but barren and contentious woman into a princess who knew how to laugh with God over the impossibilities of life that became possibilities with God!

Is there humor like this in your life? In your home? Is contention fading fast as the laughter grows? Are you learning to laugh with God over his promises, over babies born, vows kept, old age, nicknames, and spiritual growth?

Yes, God laughs at our rebellion, at our redemption, and at the routine of life.

God laughs at the resurrection. Psalm 126 says it so well: "When the Lord restored the fortunes of Zion, we were like those who dream. Then our mouth was filled with laughter, and our tongue with shouts of joy!" (vv. 1-2a).

Just think of it! From the cross, God saw man at his worst — snarling, thirsty for blood, trying to crucify God. But on the cross, man sees God at his best — loving, forgiving, appealing, hurting so we won't have to. The joy of it all is that it didn't end in the graveyard, but began there in the early morning resurrection of the third day!

A few years ago, there was an explosion and cave-in at a West Virginia coal mine. Sixteen miners were trapped in the choking dust of the blackened tunnel. Helplessly, they huddled, trying to dig their own way out. The air ebbed away. All talk ceased. Three days without food or water passed. The hole stunk with the smell of human excrement. Death couldn't be far away. All hope was spent. When suddenly, the big rocks moved and light and air penetrated their tomb. Those above had dug them out! And what a sight it was when sixteen men walked out of that mine. The news cameras were there. So were the wives and children of the miners. Such joy and laughter I have seldom seen!

This is our response to Easter as we realize God has dug us out of sin and the grave. He's rolled away the stone of death and let us loose with new life in the Spirit!

During the Middle Ages, Christians used to gather in the cathedral on Easter morning to hear the story of the resurrection read from scripture. Their response was the *risus paschalis* or "holy laughter of joy." We sing a congregational hymn today. They also shared a congregational laugh! God made it all possible.

We can laugh with God at rebellion. We can laugh with him at redemption and the things of everyday life. We can even laugh at the resurrection of Christ the Lord.

God laughs at our security. Job 5:17-27 tells it so well. Bound up as we are in the grace and power of God, who or what is there to fear? How can we ever be insecure again? "At destruction and famine you shall laugh ..." (Job 5:22).

A few years ago, television aired its doomsday film, *The Day After*, all about a nuclear war and life in the aftermath. Psychiatrists warned viewers not to watch it alone. Schools urged parental discretion. After the film, a team of experts discussed our options, yet it became all too clear that none of them had the answers. Smack in the middle of the film was the answer. The theme song for the movie was for many nothing but a lilting, haunting strain of beauty amidst death and destruction. But Christians knew it to be the tune of one of our favorite hymns, "How Firm A Foundation." It gives us the answer to *The Day After*. You see, our security is not in man's efforts for nuclear disarmament, but in God's effort to disarm sin and conquer death for all those who receive him. Christ has already done this for me and for you. In the midst of life's madness, "How firm! How firm a foundation!" As Job 41:28-29 says, "The arrow cannot make him flee; for him slingstones are turned to stubble. Clubs are counted as stubble; he laughs at the rattle of javelins." For we are secure in the love and provisions of Jesus Christ.

What Godly Laughter Can Do For Us

What have we seen so far? Some people laugh at everything. Others laugh at nothing. But the wise Christian laughs with God at his security, at the rebellious, at redemption, the resurrection, and the routine of life.

A lubricant. Just as an automobile needs oil to keep its moving parts from burning up, so humor can keep human friction at a minimum. That is one of the benefits of laughter.

No one used humor in a more lubricating, mature manner than President Ronald Reagan did. Threatening to veto any senate tax hike, he challenged, "Go ahead! Make my day!" Laughing at his age and need for a regular nap, he explained, "Russian leaders take naps, too. They just don't wake up." It all created a more agreeable, relaxed atmosphere in which to make the tough decisions of state. And believe you me, a little banter, a little teasing would go a long way in helping us get along better with the children, the office help, the neighbors, and such.

> *A glad heart makes a cheerful countenance, but by sorrow of heart the spirit is broken. All the days of the afflicted are evil, but a cheerful heart has a continual feast.* — Proverbs 15:13-15

A healer. Did you know that laughter also has the power to heal? Proverbs 17:22 says, "A cheerful heart doeth good like a medicine."

Norman Cousins was told he had an incurable illness and was given a few months to live. Cousins refused to believe it, checked himself out of the hospital and into a motel room, where he began to sort out his life. It was there that he began to watch old television reruns of humorous movies. Noticing how much better he felt after such cheerful features, he began to order videos of every funny film he could find. As the stress began to loosen, a relaxed and healed Norman Cousins emerged to write a book about it titled, *Let Me Tell You About My Non-operation*.

Medical experts have begun to discover that laughter not only relieves tension, it aids digestion, lowers blood pressure, stimulates the heart and endocrine system, activates the brain's creative center, strengthens muscles, soothes arthritic pain, and makes one more alert.

For more than eighty years, doctors have been studying negative emotions — worry, depression, guilt, self-hatred, anger, hostility, and the like. Now, some of them are beginning to study positive emotions, laughter being one of them. They are amazed at their findings. They are so amazed that many hospitals are beginning to maintain "humor rooms" where patients can go for regular doses of entertainment and cheer to speed the healing process.

Courage. Not only is humor a lubricant and healer, it is also a form of courage.

Some situations in life are so impossibly bad that the only adequate way we can deal with them is laughter. Michel Morreset ministers in Haiti amidst the poverty, the voodoo, and the ignorance. He says, "When things get really bad and we can't do anything about it, we laugh."

During World War II, an Allied general found himself surrounded during the Battle of the Bulge. The German commander sent and asked for his surrender, to which the general replied, "Nuts!"

When Alan Shepherd, the first American astronaut in space, was sitting atop an Atlas rocket ready to be blasted into outer space, the atmosphere was tense. Would the rocket explode? Others had. Shepherd dealt humorously by asking where the bathroom was. When told there was none, Shepherd went in his pants. Thus did a great American hero rocket into space laughing over a routine function of the human body.

"He laughs at the rattle of javelins," Job says in 41:29. He is courageous in the face of woe and he can laugh.

Conclusion

What about you and your sense of humor? Do you laugh at nothing? Or are you one of those who laughs at everything?

Certainly every twenty-first-century Christian's survival kit should include in it a sense of humor. To know the season when laughter with God is beautiful in its own time — that's the secret! And what better time to learn to laugh than on Easter day! For "when the Lord restored the fortunes of Zion ... then our mouth was filled with laughter!"

Suggested Prayer
Lord Jesus, help me to take you more seriously, myself less seriously, and learn to laugh hard and often with you. Amen.

---

1. William Shakespeare, *The Merchant of Venice*, Act 1, Scene 1.

Psalm 127

The Mattress Gospel

It is in vain that you rise up early and go late to rest, eating the bread of anxious toil; for he gives to his beloved sleep. — Psalm 127:2

"Uneasy lies the head that wears a crown." The King of England cannot sleep. He struts and frets upon the stage and complains, "How many thousand of my poorest subjects are at this hour asleep! Oh, sleep, gentle sleep, nature's soft nurse, how have I frightened thee that thou no more wilt weigh my eyelids down and steep my senses in forgetfulness?" That's Act 3, Scene 1 of William Shakespeare's *King Henry IV, Part 2*. But this act, this sleepless scene, is dramatized over and over again each night in thousands of bedrooms around the world. Uneasy lies the head of twenty-first-century man.

A news reporter asked a German pastor visiting Williamsburg what impressed him most about Americans. He replied, "You are a tired people. Shopkeepers, waitresses, mechanics, teachers, housewives — you look like a people desperately seeking rest, but afraid of it like a little child is afraid of naptime." As unflattering as his remark may be, it seems to have a good deal of truth in it. If you do not believe people have problems with sleep, watch television in the evening. Drug companies buy expensive prime time to commercialize sleeping pills like Lunesta, Nytol, and Ambien. According to recent figures, it takes more than 21 million sleeping pills to lull the United States to sleep on medicine designed to help them doze off. An estimated fifty million Americans suffer from sleep disorders.

What does the Bible have to say about sleep? Is it silent about something that we spend one-third of our lives doing? The average person will spend 122 days sleeping in the next year. What does the gospel teach about those days? Is there a gospel for the land of Nod?

The text says that God "gives to his beloved sleep." This is just one of the many places where the Lord intimates his concern for our slumber. If we follow this theme throughout the Bible, we can easily build a wholesome view of Christian sleep.

The Mental Dimensions Of Sleep

First, let us examine the dimensions of mental sleep. Have you ever heard this complaint? "I get out of bed more tired than when I went to bed, and I am so ill lately. I keep thinking I've been getting up on the wrong side of the bed, but left or right side, it makes no difference. I am grumpy just the same." Probably the reason for morning fatigue is not due to which side of the bed we get out of but what we do, we are in bed. Too often we go to sleep and our minds work from midnight until dawn. There is a sign on a hotel in battlefield park in Vicksburg, Mississippi, that says, "Stay with us tonight and sleep on the battleground." That's it for many people today, isn't it? They go to sleep with a civil war raging inside them. Their mattress becomes a battleground. They toss and turn all night, kick the blankets on the floor, grind their teeth until their jaws ache, and pummel their pillow like a boxer. In the morning, the entire bed is a wreck and so is the sleepless soldier of misfortune.

The scripture gives us a lifestyle that brings us to bed without such mental conflicts. God has a way of ending our inner civil wars so we can go to sleep in peace. The Lord's technique is called confession and forgiveness. It is called a clear conscience.

Each night before retiring, we should take time to make peace with the creator and the creation. It is a good time to confess your sins to the Lord, asking him to take away your guilt. You see, a guilty conscience can ravish you all night long. Our consciences are like a big bully when it comes to guilt. They get us down and twist our arms until we give in and cry, "Uncle!" The Bible says, "Agree with God, and be at peace" (Job 22:21). Each night as we prepare for slumber, we should get rid of the bully guilt by crying out, "Father, forgive!" Then the bully of guilt will leave us alone.

There will be no sin for him to twist our arms over. Thus, we can slumber at peace with ourselves.

Another interesting and helpful tonic for sleep is the biblical injunction, "Let not the sun go down on your anger" (Ephesians 4:26). The principle here is for us to get things straight with our neighbors on a daily basis. If we allow hate and injustice to accumulate over a period of time, the amassed, bitter prejudices will cause our sleep to become fitful. This is why the Lord's Prayer encourages us to forgive as we have been forgiven. This is why we must deal with our neighbors justly on a day-to-day basis.

Not only is our sleep affected by our mental attitude toward ourselves and our neighbors, it is also affected by our attitude toward things. A businessman went to his doctor complaining of insomnia. The doctor gave his some pills and told him to try counting sheep. The patient returned in two weeks still complaining of sleepless nights. "Did you try counting sheep?" The physician asked. "Yes," replied the businessman, "but that only made matters worse. I counted sheep until I got to 1,500. Then I began to figure so many ounces of wool per sheep could make 800 sweaters to be sold this fall. Now, who could sleep with an inventory like that?" How often that businessman's mental state is our own. We just can't turn it off at night!

Our work, our desire for achievement and financial gain drains us all night long. It robs us of sleep. The Bible says, "Sweet is the sleep of a laborer, whether he eats little or much; but the surfeit of the rich will not let him sleep" (Ecclesiastes 5:12). It is so true! If you do not have anything, then you do not worry about losing it. But if you own a lot, then you can worry about holding onto it. You can go to bed with financial figures in your mind, clutch at things all night long, and ruin your health. There has to be a better way! The Bible suggests it. Remember Job? He was rich, yet when he lost everything in a disastrous storm, he could say, "The Lord giveth and the Lord taketh away. Blessed be the name of the Lord" (Job 1:21). What an attitude toward things! "It came from God. It's going back to God, and it is his right now." If we, too, could learn to see our material possessions as gifts from the Lord, instead of things we feel we deserve, we'd worry a lot less, and sleep more soundly.

This leads us to another attitude that induces mental sleep. We are not only concerned with our relationship to ourselves, others, and things. We are helped or hindered with sleep by our relationship with God in Jesus Christ. Are you faithless or faithful? Do you distrust your heavenly Father or do you love him? Have you ever noticed how a little child can fall asleep on the floor in his own home? That child's sleep is so sound that his father can pick him up and take him to bed without awakening him. You see, in that little child's heart is love and faith. He knows he is at home. He trusts his father and his sleep is sound and undisturbed. Now, when we can match that child's trust of his earthly father with our own trust in our heavenly Father's care, then we have all the makings of sound mental sleep.

The Bible says, "He who keeps you will not slumber" (Psalm 121:3). Like the psalmist, do you believe God is alert to your affairs? Do you believe he is capable of taking care of you? If you do, you can curl up like a little child at your heavenly Father's feet each night and sleep like a baby!

Physical Slumber

Let us pass on now from mental sleep and examine the dimension of physical sleep. Here the Bible tells us to use our common sense. Psalm 32:9 says, "Be not like the horse or mule, without understanding." "Don't be a jackass," the scripture is saying. Use the head the good Lord gave you!

If you use your head, it will become obvious that the mattress you sleep on is important. If you are awakening at daybreak feeling tired all over, it could be due to your mattress. If it is too soft or worn out, your body fights to stay asleep all night long. It's no wonder you're exhausted by morning.

Few people realize just how important a mattress is. You will spend at least 122 days on your mattress next year. That's more time than you'll spend in your car seat, in your kitchen chair, and in the bathtub. The mattress is simply the place where you'll spend about one-third of your life.

Common sense, then, should tell you to buy a good mattress tailored to your needs. Don't buy a $4,000 bedroom suite, and then get cheap on the mattress and box springs. That's like putting recapped tires on a Cadillac. You don't sleep on that good-looking chest of drawers! You sleep on the mattresses; so make sure it's a good one.

It may also interest you to know that mattresses are like shoes and cars and overcoats. They do wear out and need replacing. You might check your mattress carefully and see if it has lost its firmness. See if it sags in the middle and if it is losing its shape around the edges. If so, replace it. A worn-out mattress is a thief. It pilfers sleep. And it is as torturing to your physical body as an Arabian bed of nails.

Not only does common sense tell us to check our mattresses, it also asks us to examine our eating and drinking habits. We all know that if you eat a pepperoni pizza before bedtime, you will be staring at the ceiling at 2 a.m. Anyone who guzzles a gallon of his favorite beverage before bedtime will be trotting back and forth to the restroom all night. Nutritional experts say that a person should eat like a king for breakfast, eat like a merchant for lunch, and eat like a pauper for supper. This aids the digestive processes, releases energy when it is most needed, and encourages the best sleep.

Physical education instructors also encourage us to get plenty of regular exercise. Nothing relieves tension like a good jog around the block, a game of tennis, or walk down the sidewalk. Ecclesiastes 5:12 mentions the sweet sleep of a common laborer. Good hard physical exercise has been known for a long time to induce sleep. There is passage in Leo Tolstoy's novel, *Anna Karenina*, where a wealthy nobleman cannot sleep. He is full of tension and anxiety over the affairs of his estate. In desperation, he grabs a sickle and goes into the fields with the peasants to harvest grain. All day long he toils. The work is strenuous, but he finds it exhilarating. Come nightfall, he falls fast asleep. It will be the same for you. When you feel tense and full of mental anguish, go out and exhaust yourself physically. Then you will sleep soundly.

We could go on here and examine other areas pertaining to physical sleep. We could look at things like noise levels, room temperatures, fresh air, and types of pajamas. We could even discuss some ailments that ward off sleep and require a doctor's attention. But you have enough common sense to evaluate those things. I will leave you in the hands of your own good sense.

Spiritual Sleep

Moving on, it becomes necessary to discuss one final dimension of the mechanics of good sleep, and that is spiritual sleep.

Some things in the home never cut off. The refrigerator runs constantly. So does your clock. There are parts of your body that work continuously, as well. Your heart pumps all your life. According to the scriptures, your soul, your spirit, works around the clock, also. In the Song of Solomon, the author confesses, "I slept, but my heart was awake" (5:2). Here, the Bible is teaching that our spiritual hearts are active even while we are sleeping.

A faithful Christian will want to take advantage of this fact. You ladies can put a turkey in the oven, let it bake while you sleep, and have a cooked meal upon rising. In like manner, you can swallow a piece of bread at bedtime, your stomach will work at digesting it all night, and by morning, the bread will be in your bloodstream. We can do the same thing with our hearts and God's word. We can go to bed with a promise of God on our minds, meditate on it all night long in our subconscious, and awaken with that truth built into our very souls.

The psalmist encourages this kind of meditative sleep. He says of himself, "I commune with my heart in the night; I meditate and search my spirit" (77:6). And he encourages us, saying, "Commune with your own hearts on your beds" (4:4). If you take the psalm writer's advice and meditate on God's word throughout the night, you will find your whole thought-life being reorganized. The Christian life begins with repentance, literally "a change of mind." It continues when we meditate, an act of thinking God's thoughts after him. This process of mental reorganization continues until we have left our old mind behind and taken on the mind of Christ. Our old thought patterns, attitudes, and values are kicked out and the very mind of Christ is brought in. This is what Saint Paul was talking about in Ephesians 4:22-24 when he wrote, "Put off your old nature which belongs to your former manner of life and is corrupt through deceitful lusts, and be renewed in the spirit of your minds, and put on the new nature, created after the likeness of God."

This putting off one mind and putting on another can take place in sleep. Our minds and our hearts simply work all night. It is up to us to determine how they work. We can go to bed relishing a lustful thought, fantasize sexually all night long, and awaken with adultery and fornication more strongly reinforced as a habit in our minds. But if we go to sleep thinking of the Lord, if we commune with his promises all night long, we will wake up with godly character built more solidly into our lives. The principle is quite simple here. The thoughts you carry into bed will increase and magnify during sleep. If you go to bed with lust, you will wake up with a bent toward fornication. It's like going to bed with a coat hanger in your mouth. You wake up with a smile on your face! Likewise, if you go to bed and think of God, you'll wake up more like him in the morning.

Yes, God can use slumber to give us his mind. He can also use sleep to communicate his will to us. The Bible is full of episodes where the Lord speaks to people in dreams and visions during slumber. God spoke to Abraham, Isaac, Jacob, Joseph, and Pharaoh in dreams. In the New Testament, it is recorded that the Lord spoke to Jesus' own father, Joseph, at least twice in dreams. Perhaps the first time God used sleep to communicate to man was in Genesis where the Lord caused a deep sleep to fall over Adam. Then God made Eve, awakened Adam, and gave him Eve for a wife. What a dream! (There's a cartoon that shows Adam sitting on a rock looking very tired and sleepless. God is standing by, saying, "Adam, why can't you sleep?" Adam replies, "The last time I went to sleep you brought that woman and left her here. I'm afraid to go to sleep again. I don't know what I'd do with two!")

Perhaps God uses the nighttime to speak with us because that is the only time he can slow us down enough to get our attention. At any rate, God has historically used dreams and visions to communicate with us. This does not mean every dream or vision is from God. Some are — some aren't — but when we have them, we should heed them and evaluate them strictly in terms of scripture.

The Lord does not use dreams as much today as he used to, it seems. After all, he has spoken his final word to us in Christ Jesus. But sometimes the Lord may choose to communicate to us by a dream or a nocturnal vision. My grandmother lost her mother to death back in 1963. For some months after the funeral, Grandmother wrestled with her grief. She could not seem to settle it in her mind that her loved one was safe with the Lord. One night, however, she had a beautifully vivid dream. She saw her mother standing before her, looking as healthy, alert, and happy as ever before. In the dream, her mother said, "Now, Marion, see! I am fine. Stop your worrying about me because I am with the Lord." And after that, my grandmother quit fretting and slept soundly.

Conclusion

So now we've taken a quick look at some of the things the Christian faith teaches about sleep. We have looked at mental sleep, physical sleep, and spiritual sleep. Some of you are thinking that if you tried all this, your sleep would become so structured it would seem a bureaucratic nightmare of red tape! But this is not necessarily so! All of these principles can be incorporated into your lifestyle over a period of time. These principles can become habits that are second nature to you. You will not have to think to do them. They will become automatic and so will your sleep.

A famous mattress company advertises its products with the slogan, "For the *rest* of your life!" Today the church would like to advertise the Lord the same way. Perhaps you've never thought of the Lord as a sleep merchant. But that is at least part of who he is. He can, if you will allow him, give you the rest of your life. Jesus said, "Come unto me, all you who labor and are heavy laden, and I will give you rest" (Matthew 11:28).

In case you have not noticed it yet, the gospel of sound sleep is summed up in the "Great Commandment." When you love God, your neighbor, yourself, and the creation, you are freed from the fears, the frustrations, and the attitudes that ward off sleep. When you learn to come to Jesus with faith, love him with all your mind, heart, body, and soul, he gives you rest. Isn't that something you both need and want? Then come to him! Take his yoke and learn from him! Learn to love God mind, heart, body, and soul. Learn to love yourself and your neighbor. Thereby, you will learn sleep. You'll get your fifty winks. You'll saw your ZZZZZZ's. You'll snore away in the best tradition of the sandman. Rip Van Winkle and Sleeping Beauty have nothing on you! "For he giveth his beloved sleep."

Suggested Prayer
I come to you, O Father. Forgive my sins. Give me your promised rest. Take from my neck this yoke of sin and give to me the yoke of Christ. Let me learn from him — love for God, self, people, world — let me learn it all from him. And come evening, Lord, let my rest be sound, my sleep childlike. In Jesus' name. Amen.

Psalms 120-134

Getting Away From It All To Get Back To It All

Lift up your hands to the holy place, and bless the Lord!
— Psalm 134:2

Have you ever "had it" with being involved? Have you ever wanted to quit? Have you ever been so tired of people you'd like to pinch their heads off? I have.

The Bible tells us we are not alone. In Jeremiah 9:2, the prophet lamented, "O that I had in the desert a wayfarer's lodging place, that I might leave my people." In Psalm 55:6, David yearned, "O that I had wings like a dove! I would fly away and be at rest." After the crucifixion, Peter put it more simply, "I'm going fishing" (John 21:3). Even Jesus told his disciples, "Come away and rest yourself for a while." And he led them from the crowds across the Sea of Galilee in a sailboat (Mark 6:31-32).

Webster's Dictionary defines "vacation" as "a period of rest from work, a holiday." When the Bible talks about time off from work or vacationing, it uses the word "rest," which in the Hebrew is *shabath* and means "to repose, desist from exertion, to cease, celebrate, or leave."

In the United States, Christians badly need to get a grip on vacationing and involvement. We need to develop a biblical, loving theology of leisure that sets a balance between routine community involvement on the one hand and rest and renewal on the other. We need to discover the Christian mean between overwork and underwork.

Workaholism

There are extremes. On the one hand are workaholics, self-appointed indispensables who carry the weight of the world around on their shoulders. Such people never believe it in Genesis 2:2 when almighty God took a day to rest. Equally unbelievable is Genesis 18:4 when Abraham encouraged the two Sodom-bound angels to turn aside and rest for a while and they did so! The way I operate is that if the work is there, it has to be done. God and angels may need to rest. But not me!

On Garrison Keiller's radio show, *A Prairie Home Companion*, the Catholic church is called Our Lady of Perpetual Responsibility. And what a fitting symbol such a church and lifestyle is for so many of our day who feel guilty when they rest.

I once worked an entire year in a church without a vacation. When my wife insisted that I get away, I announced my plans for a holiday to the church. The thought of my leaving the ministry totally in their hands while I went on a vacation set off a major panic in the fellowship. One of the well-meaning older saints handed me the following poem ...

> *Would the farmer leave his cattle,*
> *Or the shepherd leave his sheep?*
> *Who would give them shelter or*
> *Provide them food to eat?*
> *Did Saint Paul get such a notion?*
> *Did a Wesley or a Knox?*
> *Did they in the heat of summer*
> *Turn away their needy flocks?*
> *Did you ever know it happen,*
> *Or hear anybody tell,*
> *Satan takin' a vacation, shuttin'*
> *Up the doors of hell?*
> *So it strikes me unusual when*
> *A man of holy hands*
> *Thinks he needs a vacation to*
> *Forsake his little lambs!*

From 35 years of experience, I finally arrived at a stock answer to those who tell me I cannot have a vacation because, "The devil never takes a week off!" "Yes," I readily agree, "and that is exactly who I'd become if I didn't take some time out for rest!"

Just look at the first psalm of ascent; Psalm 120. In seven short verses, the author uses words like distress, cry, lying lips, deceitful tongue, warrior's sharp arrows, woe, war, and too long. Obviously, the man has had it with community involvement. He feels surrounded. He is little more than a negative cynic dulled by too much routine work among people.

Elijah makes a fascinating study here. The prophet worked endlessly to call Israel from waywardness. His prayer stopped the rains. His sermons enraged a king and a queen. His duel with the prophets of Baal atop Mount Carmel proved who was the real God. But then Elijah burned out and fled into the wilderness to wallow in self-pity. "And I, only I, am left!" Hear that? "It's all up to me. There is nobody left to do the work but me!" And God reminded Elijah as he must remind you and me, "I still have 5,000 prophets who have not bowed the knee to Baal." The fact is, God has thousands of workers, plenty of others who can do our jobs. And we are, none of us, as indispensable as we might think.

If you wish to conduct an experiment to see just how important you are and just how much the world will miss you when you are gone, put your hand in a bucket of water and then remove it. See the hole that is left where your hand was? That's how much the universe will miss you when you're gone.

Leisure Lifestyle

The other extreme from workaholism is being leisure-lost. And this is what our culture really pushes at us today. "Life is a beach!" It's better in the Bahamas." "You deserve a break today, so get up and get away!" The goal of this lifestyle is to earn as much money as easily and quickly as possible, retire early, and get completely uninvolved so that one may live life on one's own terms.

For some, ours is the era of the three- or four-day workweek, the long weekend, the condo, the Corvette, the club, and the hot tub. "Take the money and run!" With all this, you can see why involvement is outvoting children, marriage, meaningful and kept church covenants, and the like. We want to live unencumbered. It's like the sign I once saw on a beach cottage. It read, "Who cares?"

Our motto has become that of a popular poster adorning college walls, "You go your way and I'll go mine; you do your thing and I'll do mine. And if we meet, it's beautiful."

We have become like the children of Israel who, still without the law in the wilderness, turned away from the Lord to worship creation — gold, wine, foreign women, and self. Of them and us, Exodus 32:6 reports, "The people sat down to eat and drink and rose up to play."

I need to remind you that the way of the kingdom of God is opposite the way of our modern culture. Society says, "Blessed are those who are independent, who've got it all together, who've got it made!" Christ said, "Blessed are the poor in spirit."

Society says, "Blessed are those who are carefree, who don't give a damn, and who know how to party!" Jesus said, "Blessed are those who mourn."

Our society says, "Blessed are those who are not restrained by obligations and morals. Live it up! If it feels good, do it!" The Lord said, "Blessed are those who hunger and thirst after righteousness."

Our culture says, "Blessed are the powerful, the influential, and the bosses who always get their way. Flaunt it!" Christ said, "Blessed are the meek."

Our day says, "Blessed are the compromisers, those who fit in comfortably, and who don't make waves." Jesus said, "Blessed are those who are persecuted for righteousness sake."

And what we're left with is an individual devoid of any community benefit, a self-centered egomaniac, undependable, uninvolved, always gone after his next pleasure — leisure-lost.

God's Balance

In between all of this workaholism and hedonism is God's balance, the balance the Bible calls "sabbath" or rest — the balance that comes in the tension between involvement and getting away from it all.

Most assuredly such a balance does not come naturally to the Christian. Jeremiah 31:2 says we must seek such a rest. Joshua 1:13 says only God gives it. Isaiah 11:10 says such a rest is glorious. And Hebrews 4:11 warns us sternly, "Let us therefore strive to enter that rest, that no one fall by ... disobedience."

God designed a delightfully meaningful way for his people to live rested in the tension between community involvement and vacations. About five or six times a year there was a great Jewish festival in Jerusalem. All the tribes of Israel were encouraged to take time off from work and go up for the feast of the Passover or Pentecost or the Feast of Trumpets, Atonement, or Tabernacles.

This meant a happy pilgrimage, a walk through the countryside, and camping out. It meant food and laughter, music, dancing, and a change of pace and scenery. Finally, in Jerusalem, at Mount Zion, it meant worship.

The abiding principles here for you and for me are obvious. Five or six times a year, we, too, need to take a few days off from work and enjoy a God-ordained break in our routines. Budgeting five or six times will keep us from workaholism on the one hand as well as vacationing endlessly on the other.

Such a plan also calls for periodic vacationing — not taking the entire summer off, but vacations strategically spaced throughout the year. In the past, I've worked until I'm all but spent. Then I panic and look at my schedule book and find that it is ten weeks before I can extract myself for three days. So I spend ten weeks fatigued, grouchy, and less than ably doing my job. God's way is better. Every few months comes a planned break, a holiday to be anticipated. And by so spacing them, by so scheduling them into our lifestyles, we get away from it all when we need to, not afterward.

Note well that God's idea of a holiday was not darting to the beach to oversleep, overeat, overspend, and carouse with indulgent people who do not share his name or community. Jewish vacations involved music, dancing, and a long walk. They were treks taking city folks and villagers "back to nature." The psalms of ascent are full of references to the great outdoors — mountains, trees, the sun, moon, stars, and grass.

Note also that their vacations never took them more than seventy miles from home. Jerusalem could be reached from any point in the country by a few days of walking.

A professional man I know suffered a heart attack in his late forties. His life was a fast-paced whirl of workaholism on the weekdays and hedonism on the weekends. (Some of us manage to live both extremes, you know.) Monday through Friday, 7 a.m. to 6 p.m., he worked like a dervish. Then on the weekend, he'd head for either his mountain cabin or his beach cottage, either one a stressful 200-mile drive away. After his heart attack, he confessed to me, "I just pushed my body so hard at work and at play that it broke down due to lack of *rest*."

Certainly, "rest" need not be all that great an expense and distance away. God benevolently placed all his children needed close at hand, within easy walking distance, and at an affordable price. I just bet if you but look close to home, you, too, will find the good Lord providing for your needs as well.

Notice also that godly vacations have worship at their center. Jerusalem, Mount Zion, almighty God, and the everlasting covenant, were the focal point of their holiday journeyings. Praise, singing, fellowship, and worship were a part of every step. Contrast that with a lady, who while reveling bawdily at the beach, excused herself, saying, "When I come to the beach, I leave my religion at the county line."

Now, if you will, compare God's idea of vacationing with man's current notions and see the difference.

God's View	Man's View
Rest oriented	Leisure oriented
Receive oriented	"Do" oriented
Readily available, close by	Someplace else, must travel
Free of charge	Costly
Available to all	Available to the rich
God-made	Man-made
Produces love, routine, involvement, and dependability	Produces selfishness, lack of routine, no dependability or involvement

Lasting	A quick fix, wears off, leaves one always wanting more
Brings rest, revival, renewal	Brings fatigue
Fosters contentment	Brings discontentment
Engenders a seven-day week mentality, a sense of propriety	Engenders a "weekend" mentality
Emphasizes individualism in community	Destroys community

Conclusion

There you have it. Workaholism on the one extreme, a leisure lifestyle on the other — and God's rest perfectly balanced between the two.

What we have in these fifteen psalms of ascent encompassing Psalms 120-134 is a record of "going up" from the routine workaday life of the village to the sublime climates of a holiday in the holy city. These psalms are much like Chaucer's *Canterbury Tales*. They are pilgrim songs — vacationers' hymns.

Some say each of these songs were sung on one of the fifteen steps leading from the outer courts to the inner court of the temple itself. Others say they were sung at fifteen different stages of return from Babylonian captivity. Others recognize them as all these things and more. They were a handbook of devotions for Jerusalem bound pilgrims. Carried in small scrolls, known by heart by adults, they were songs sung around the campfires and along the highways as people traveled to Jerusalem to celebrate a feast.

Jesus would have sung these very same songs. After all, he made the trip to Jerusalem many times. A detailed account of his "going up" with his parents when he was twelve years old is included in the gospels.

Notice how they begin in Psalm 120 with fatigue, negativism, and hurt. "Deliver me, O Lord, from lying lips, from a deceitful tongue."

Then in Psalm 121 the journey begins toward Mount Zion. "I will lift up my eyes unto the hills. From whence does my help come? My help comes from the Lord."

Psalm 122 has the pilgrim in Jerusalem, poised and ready to enter the temple. "I was glad when they said to me, 'Let us go into the house of the Lord.'"

Then in Psalm 123, he sees the Lord, is comforted in all of life's trials. "Behold, as the eyes of servants look to the hands of their master ... so our eyes look to the Lord our God."

In Psalm 124, the pilgrim feels gratitude. In Psalm 125, he feels secure in the Lord as he begins to trudge homeward. Psalm 126 is about laughter. In Psalm 127, the pilgrim is thinking about the community he will build after arrives home. Psalms 128 through 133 are occupied with thoughts of family, hope, patience, rethinking one's heritage, and community togetherness.

By the time the psalms of ascent end with 134, just look at the attitude change from Psalm 120! In Psalm 120, he is negative. He has his eyes on man and sin, but in Psalm 134 he has his eyes on God and invites us all, "Come! Take a break. Come bless the Lord, all you servants of the Lord!"

Quite literally, he has gotten away from it all so he could get back to it all. When he left, life seemed like a problem, but when he returned, life seemed like an opportunity.

Suggested Prayer
Dear God, please grant each of us the opportunity to seek and find such divine rest in this leisure-lost world of ours today. Amen.

Afterword

Let us remember ... that in the end we go to poetry for one reason, so that we might more fully inhabit our lives and the world in which we live them, and that if we more fully inhabit these things, we might be less apt to destroy both.
— Christian Wiman

It is difficult to get the news from poems yet men die miserably every day for lack of what is found there.
— From *Asphodel, that Greeny Flower*

www.ingramcontent.com/pod-product-compliance
Lightning Source LLC
Chambersburg PA
CBHW071708040426
42446CB00011B/1970